FORWARD

Welcome...
An amazing world of food and nutrition, coupled with extraordinary culinary insight is about to unfold.

When we marry tradition with state-of-the-art function, the result is an appliance for the next generation of food and family lovers. If you've ever sat around grandma's kitchen, as wonderful aromas of warm spices and slow cooking meals brought amazing memories of family and friends, then NuWave has a cooking appliance for you.

We worked incredibly hard to perfect the Nutri-Pot Electric Pressure Cooker. Safety was foremost in our minds as we developed the Nutri-Pot and with our Sure Lock system our team delivered. I get to enjoy countless hours in our test Kitchen, developing literally hundreds of recipes with my amazing Culinary Team, to share with you. Here are 200 to get you started in the ease and amazing nutritional benefits of pressure cooking.

Grandma knew a few things about food and family; she knew how to feed us sometimes quickly and nutritiously. She knew how to cook on a budget and how to use the incredible science of pressure cooking to deliver amazing budget-friendly meals.

Well, we took notes from Grandmas around the country and applied them to our amazing Nutri-Pot.

Now like never before has time saving, nutrition, and safety come together.

We'll explore cuisines from around the world with fully tested and authentic recipes reflecting my 30 years as an award-winning chef and Culinary School instructor. There are no gimmicks in these pages like you might see in others. There are no silly unhealthy meals that do not reflect your passion for cooking. We listened to everyday folks, chefs, and even former students of mine to make sure we developed authentic recipes for you and your family.

Have an amazing journey with your family and friends, and remember to "Live Well For Less".

David Oland, CEC
NuWave Executive Chef

TABLE OF CONTENTS

Quick Start	5
Pressure Cooking Notes	8
Introduction	9
Measurement Chart	10
Soups, Stews & Sauces	11
Rice, Grains & Pastas	57
Meats	100
Seafood	189
Vegetables & Sides	209
Desserts	249
Canning	271
Recipe Index	282
Our Products	284

QUICK START

Main Display Interface

Presets

Presets

Functions

Press once to start or stop.
Press twice to clear.

When properly locked, the LED icon will light up to show that the SURE LOCK™ feature is active.

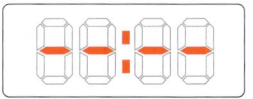 When unit is not cooking, or when no function has been selected, the LED screen will display "--:--", indicating that the unit is not in operation.

Preset Example:

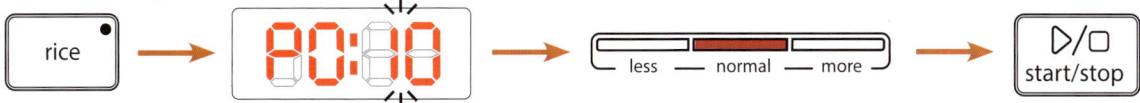

Follow these simple steps for each Preset. For this example, **"P0:10"** is the default pressure time. The pressure time will vary depending on the preset you choose.

Functions Example:

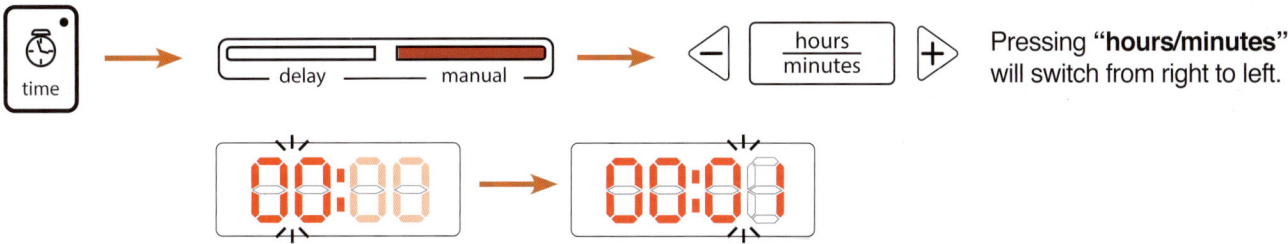

Pressing **"hours/minutes"** will switch from right to left.

Time: This function lets you manually adjust the cooking time, overriding the default Presets and Functions.

QUICK START

Default Times

Below are the default, minimum, and maximum times for the Functions and Presets. For more detailed instructions on the Presets and Functions, please refer to the Pressure Cooker Manual.

Default Time		Texture (minutes)			Time (minutes & hours)	
Presets & Functions	**Hours : Minutes**	**Less**	**Normal**	**More**	**Min.***	**Max**
Rice	00:10	00:07	00:10	00:13	00:01	01:40
Multi Grain	00:27	00:22	00:27	00:32	00:01	01:40
Soup	00:15	00:10	00:15	00:20	00:01	01:40
Meat/Stew	00:40	00:20	00:40	00:50	00:01	01:40
Poultry	00:20	00:15	00:20	00:25	00:01	01:40
Beans	00:20	00:15	00:20	00:25	00:01	01:40
Fish	00:08	00:06	00:08	00:10	00:01	01:40
Steam/Veggies	00:05	00:03	00:05	00:07	00:01	01:40
Potatoes	00:06	00:04	00:06	00:10	00:01	01:40
Bake	00:40	00:30	00:40	00:50	00:01	01:40
Canning	00:20				00:01	01:40
Delay					00:05	24:00
Warm	04:00				01:00	24:00
Sear	00:05				00:01	00:20
Slow Cook	04:00				02:00	09:00

*Minimum Time

● Default Times   ● Texture Times   ● Adjustable Times

Note: This function lets you manually adjust the cooking time, overriding the default Presets and Functions.

Delay: Manages how slow you want the cook time to be set.

Warm: Keeps your food warm after cooking. Refer to the Auto Warm Times chart on the next page.

Sear: Browns food quickly at high temperatures.

Slow Cook: Ideal for soups and stews.

For more information on all Presets and Functions please refer to the Owner's Manual.

⚠ CAUTION

a) A short power-supply cord should be provided to reduce risks resulting from becoming entangled in or tripping over a longer cord.

b) Longer detachable power-supply cords are available and may be used if care is exercised in their use.

c) If a long detachable power-supply cord is used:
   1) The marked electrical rating of the detachable power-supply cord should be at least as great as the electrical rating of the unit;
   2) If the unit is of the grounded type, the extension cord should be a grounding type 2-wire cord; and
   3) The longer cord should be arranged so that it will not drape over the countertop or tabletop where it can be pulled on by children or tripped over unintentionally.

QUICK START

Auto Warm Times

The NuWave Nutri-Pot® Digital Pressure Cooker is programmed to a set pressure of 70kPa. **kPa** as a unit of pressure measurement, is widely used throughout the world instead of the **"Pounds per Square Inch, (PSI)"** method. The kPa to PSI ratio is approximately 7kPa to 1PSI. **For example: 2PSI is equal to 14kPa.**

Presets	Auto Warm Feature		
	Indefinitely	Auto Shutoff	Time Hours: Minutes
Rice	✓		
Multi Grain			
Soup	✓		04:00
Meat/Stew			02:00
Poultry			01:00
Beans			04:00
Fish			
Steam/Veggies			
Potatoes			01:00
Bake	✓		
Canning	✓		
Warm (Function)			04:00

Rice, Soup, Bake, and Canning functions are set to Auto Warm Indefinitely. Soup has a starting point of 4 minutes if set to warm manually.

Meat/Stew, Poultry, Beans, and Potatoes have their default times when setting to warm manually.

Minimum & Maximum Amounts

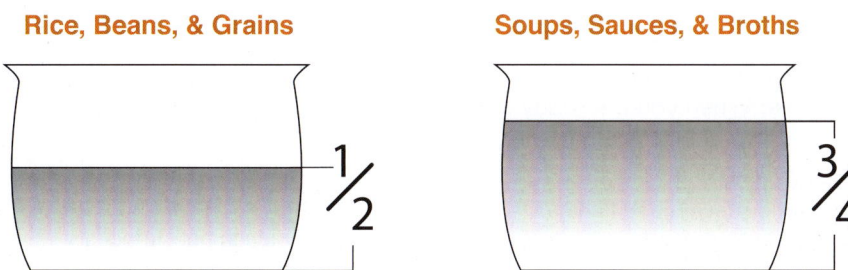

Rice, Beans, & Grains — 1/2

Soups, Sauces, & Broths — 3/4

For rice, beans, and grains, do not fill more than half full.

For soups, sauces, and broths do not fill more than ¾ full.

Overfilling may risk clogging the vent pipes and developing excess pressure. This could also cause spillage and may damage to the unit. The total amount of food and water should NEVER exceed the maximum level marking of the inner pot. Please refer to the max fill lines in the inner pot.

PRESSURE COOKING NOTES

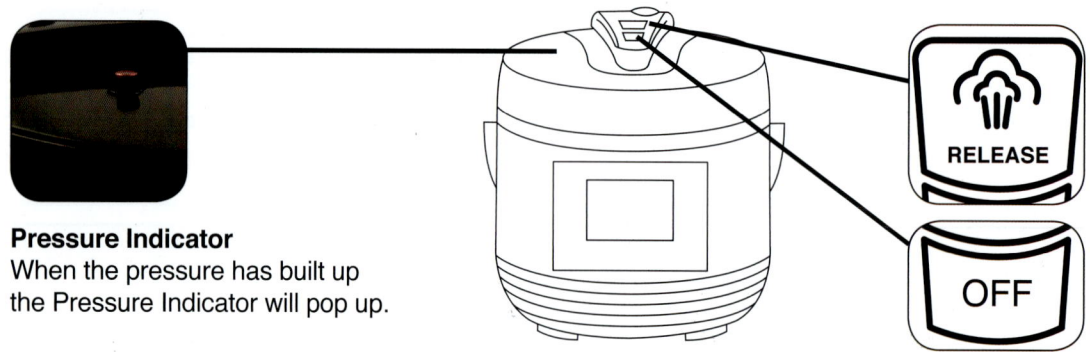

Pressure Indicator
When the pressure has built up the Pressure Indicator will pop up.

Pressure Cooking

Tip: The NuWave Nutri-Pot Digital Pressure Cooker will beep to indicate that the cooking time is complete.

Preheating: While the unit reaches the appropriate temperature for the function selected, the display will show "PH", indicating that it is preheating. Once the unit reaches the appropriate pressure, it will shift from preheating to the selected preset cooking time. Once pressure has built inside the pressure cooker, the "PH" displayed will change to "P", followed by the amount of time it will remain under pressure.

Pressure: The function selected will determine the amount of pressure time. For example, the display will show "P0:10" (pressure time). The colon or ":" will flash to indicate that the pressure cooker is under pressure and the timer is counting down.

Auto Warm Feature: When pressure cooking is complete, the pressure cooker will automatically switch to the "warm" function. This allows the pressure to naturally release while your food remains warm.

What is quick release? To quickly release the pressure, simply press down the "Pressure Release Button". The button will stay down and steam will be rapidly released. When the Floater Valve next to the Pressure Release Valve, as well as the Pressure Indicator has dropped, indicating pressure has been properly released, you can then safely open the pressure cooker.

What is natural release? To naturally release the pressure, simply wait for the Floater Valve and the Pressure Indicator to drop. Doing so will allow the pressure cooker to naturally release steam as it slowly cools. This allows you to finish the cooking process as the pressure cooker gradually releases steam. The natural release method can take up to 45 minutes. **If any pressure remains in the pressure cooker, simply press the "Pressure Release Button" for a quick release of any remaining pressure and follow the remaining steps for "quick release."**
Resuming Pressure: When you are ready to cook under pressure, press the "OFF" button. If the "Pressure Release Button" is down, the pressure cannot build up.

IMPORTANT SAFEGUARDS

1. **Do not touch hot surfaces.** Use handle.
2. To protect against electrical shock, do not immerse cord, plugs, or the unit in water or other liquid.
3. Close supervision is necessary when any unit is used by or near children.
4. Unplug from outlet when not in use and before cleaning. Allow unit to cool before adding on or removing off parts.
5. Do not operate any unit with a damaged cord or plug, after the unit malfunctions or it has been damaged in any manner. **In case the unit is malfunctioning, please contact Customer Service at 1-877-6889-2838 or via email help@nuwavenow.com.**
6. The use of other accessories that are not intended to be used with this unit is not recommended. Doing so may damage the unit and can cause accidents.
7. **NOT INTENDED FOR OUTDOOR USE.**
8. Do not let cord hang over edge of table or counter, or touch hot surfaces.
9. Do not place on or near a hot gas or electric burner and or in a heated oven.
10. Extreme caution must be used when moving a unit containing hot oil or other hot liquids.
11. Always attach the plug to the unit first, then plug the cord into the wall outlet.
12. To disconnect, turn any control "OFF", then remove plug from the wall outlet.
13. **DO NOT place any object above the pressure release Valve. This is where steam is being released from the NuWave Nutri-Pot® Digital Pressure Cooker.**
14. **DO NOT USE THE UNIT FOR OTHER THAN INTENDED USE.**

INTRODUCTION

Understanding how it works:
The recipes in this book were designed for the 6-quart NuWave Nutri-Pot® pressure cooker. All the ingredients can fit into our larger pressure cookers using the same time.

Building pressure and cooking under pressure:
When using the NuWave Nutri-Pot pressure cooker you will see two steps, PH and P(number).

PH – Once you enter in the time you want your food to cook at, the pressure cooker will show a "PH", indicating that it is building up to pressure.

P(number) – Once the pressure cooker has built the appropriate amount of pressure, it will automatically start the countdown for you. When it is done, it will automatically stop cooking under pressure so you can quick release or let it naturally release.

Pressure information:
All the recipes developed were with our NuWave Pressure Cooker that is programmed to set a pressure of 70kPa or 10.15PSI. kPa is a unit of pressure measurement.

7kPa=1PSI:
Pressure cookers work by building pressure based on an amount of liquid heated to create steam. The steam is safely trapped in the unit, which creates the high-pressure atmosphere. We recommend, if you've never used an electric pressure cooker, to place ½ qt of water in your unit, lock the lid, and turn it on any of the preset buttons. The unit will preheat, and when the right pressure is achieved, it will begin the timed cooking process.

All of the presets and time function have the same pressure, just a difference in the length of time it will cook. So, don't be nervous, let's get some water in the Nutri-Pot and get cooking. Always follow the measurements in your recipes and the liquid amount, also carefully follow times.

Building and releasing pressure: quick release vs. natural release
What is quick release? To quickly release the pressure, simply press the "Pressure Release Button". Once the pressure is completely released, you can then safely open the pressure cooker.

What is natural release? To naturally release the pressure, simply wait for the pressure to release from the pressure cooker. This can take up to 45 minutes. If any pressure remains in the pressure cooker, simply press the "Pressure Release Button" to release any remaining pressure.

Always use caution when removing the lid. Steam is very hot.

Canning:
Before pressure canning, always consult an instructional book written specifically for pressure canning. The NuWave pressure cooker goes up to 70kPa and can be used for basic pressure cooking high-acidic foods, along with the water bath method. Meat and seafood are not recommended. Consult your manual for more details.

Slow cooking and warming:
All of your slow cooker recipes can be used in the Nutri-Pot with our available slow cooker lid. Use our warm feature to hold food for dinner later, or use as a buffet with our slow cooker lid. This function will let you manually adjust the time you would like to keep your food warm. The NuWave Nutri-Pot pressure cooker will automatically go to this warm function when a desired preset has completed. Refer to the manual for more details. NuWave really wants you to "Live Well For Less" and we've achieved that with Nutri-Pot. The nutritional benefits of Nutri-Pot cooking as well as the benefits to your wallet and allowing more time with your family are things we can all come around the table for.

Enjoy cooking!

David Oland, CEC
NuWave Executive Chef

MEASUREMENT CHART

Teaspoon = t	**Fahrenheit = °F**	**Minute = min**
Tablespoon = T	**Celsius = °C**	**Second = sec**
Cup = c	**Fluid Ounces = fl oz**	**Inch = in.**
Ounce = oz	**Liter = L**	**Dozen = doz**
Pound = lb(s)	**Milliliter = ml**	**Hour = hr**
Quart = qt	**Package = pkg.**	**Gram = g**
Pint = pt	**Gallon = gal**	

SOUPS, STEWS & SAUCES

Beef Barley Soup 12
Bone Broth for Health 13
Tuscan White Bean Soup with
Swiss Chard & Smoked Ham 15
Classic Clam Chowder
with New Potatoes 16
Cream of Chicken
with Wild Rice 17
Turkey Soup (From
Thanksgiving Leftovers) 18
Creamless Cauliflower Soup with
Yukon Gold Potatoes 20
Italian Wedding Soup
with Baby Meatballs 21
Nacho Cheese Sauce
for Game Day 23
Pork Pozole with Hominy 24
Chicken Soup with
Farro & Vegetables 25
Black Bean Soup
with Cotija Cheese 27
Carrot-Ginger Soup 28
Marinara Sauce (Traditional) 29
Black Bean Soup with
Toasted Cumin & Cilantro 31

Minestrone Soup 32
Split Pea Soup with Ham 33
Borscht 35
Bourbon Street Gumbo with
Shrimp & Andouille 36
Chickpeas with
Tomatoes 37
Texas Beef Chili 39
Potato Leek Soup 40
Beef Burgundy with
Root Vegetables & Red Wine 41
Chicken & Dumpling Soup 43
Butternut Squash Soup 44
Homemade Vegetable Soup 45
Lentil Soup 46
Pho Ga 47
Corn & Mushroom Soup 49
Chicken Tortilla Soup 51
Soup of the Seven Seas 52
Tomato Basil Bisque
with Herb Croutons 53
Ditalini Soup 54
Tom Ka Gai 55

Soups, Stews & Sauces

BEEF BARLEY SOUP

Serves 6

Ingredients:

- 2t olive oil
- 3lbs stew beef (chuck or pot roast)
- 1 onion, diced medium
- 2 carrots, peeled, diced large
- ¼c celery, diced
- 8oz mushrooms, sliced
- 1T tomato paste
- 1T Worcestershire sauce
- ½t freshly ground black pepper
- 1c pearl barley, rinsed, drained
- 4c chicken stock

Instructions:

1. Set to "sear" and add oil.
2. When oil is hot, add beef and sauté for 4 minutes. When done, remove beef; set aside.
3. Add onions, celery, carrots, and mushrooms and sauté for 4 minutes.
4. Add tomato paste and Worcestershire sauce.
5. Add barley, chicken stock, and return beef.
6. Close lid and lock. Set to "soup" and adjust for 10 minutes.
7. When done, natural release for 35 minutes. Afterward, quick release until all pressure is released.
8. Open and ladle soup into bowls. Serve with hearty bread.

Soups, Stews & Sauces

BONE BROTH
FOR HEALTH

Serves 6

Ingredients:

- 4½ lbs beef bones (mix of marrow, knuckle, and meat bones)
- 6 sprigs thyme
- 2T apple cider vinegar
- 2 carrots, quartered
- 1 onion, halved
- 2 celery stalks, diced
- 4 garlic cloves
- 1 bay leaf

Instructions:

1. Preheat regular oven to 400°F. Place bones on a roasting tray. Roast in oven for 30 minutes.
2. Transfer bones and fat to pressure cooker with remaining ingredients.
3. Add enough water to cover the bones (pressure cooker must not be more than ⅔ full).
4. Close lid and lock. Set to "slow cook" for 4 hours.
5. When done, natural release for 35 minutes. Afterward, quick release until all pressure is released.
6. Open lid, carefully remove inner pot, and gently stir. Strain into a large bowl. Cool bowl (with liquid) by placing in a sink or a large tub filled with ice water. Remove bay leaf. Discard hard layer of fat.

Soups, Stews & Sauces

TUSCAN WHITE BEAN SOUP
WITH SWISS CHARD & SMOKED HAM

Serves 4

Ingredients:

- 1T olive oil
- 2-3 smoked ham shanks or hocks
- 1 large onion, diced
- 4 cloves garlic, minced
- 3 carrots, peeled, sliced
- 1 (16-oz) package small white beans, soaked overnight (or use quick-soak method)
- 1t basil
- 1t oregano
- 1t thyme
- ½t fennel
- 1t red pepper flakes
- ½t mustard powder
- 2 bay leaves
- 1T Worcestershire sauce
- 3T sherry vinegar
- 1T honey
- 1 (32-oz) pkg. vegetable, chicken, or beef broth
- 1 (26-oz) can tomatoes
- 3c water
- 1 large bunch Swiss chard, stems removed, cleaned, and chopped
- Sea salt and freshly ground pepper to taste
- Parmesan cheese

Instructions:

1. Set to "sear" and add oil. Add ham and lightly brown.
2. Add onions and carrots and sauté until onions are translucent. Add garlic and sauté for an additional 1-2 minutes.
3. Add basil, oregano, thyme, fennel, red pepper flakes, and mustard powder. Stir to coat the vegetables and meat.
4. Add tomatoes, broth, Worcestershire sauce, vinegar, honey, and bay leaves. Stir.
5. Add white beans and water. Season with sea salt and fresh ground black pepper to taste.
6. Place Swiss chard on top of beans. Stir for 1 minute so chard wilts down. Ensure the contents are not going over the maximum fill line.
7. Close lid and lock. Set to "soup" and adjust for 12 minutes.
8. When done, natural release for 35 minutes. Afterward, quick release until all pressure is released.
9. Open. Remove ham and bay leaves. Let cool slightly.
10. Remove meat from the bones.
11. Add meat back into soup. Stir.
12. Top with freshly grated Parmesan cheese. Serve.

Soups, Stews & Sauces

CLASSIC CLAM CHOWDER
WITH NEW POTATOES

Serves 4

Ingredients:

- 3 (10¼- to 14-oz) cans of clams, minced
- ½ lb lean bacon (reserve some for garnish) or ½ lb salt pork, diced
- 1c onions, diced
- 3c raw potatoes, diced, peeled
- 1t sea salt
- ¼t white pepper
- 2c half and half
- 2c milk
- 2T butter
- Paprika
- 1 sprig fresh thyme (optional)

Instructions:

1. Drain clams and reserve liquid.
2. Measure the clam juice, adding enough water to make 4c of liquid; set aside.
3. Set to "sear", add bacon, and sauté until browned. Remove bacon; set aside on folded paper towels.
4. Drain off all but ¼ of the fat and add onions. Sauté for several minutes.
5. Add potatoes, sea salt, white pepper, and reserved clam liquid (mixed with water), and bring up to a boil.
6. Close lid and lock. Set to "soup" for 10 minutes.
7. When done, quick release until all pressure is released. (If you do a natural release, pressure cooker will automatically go into "warm" to keep soup hot; add final ingredients when you are closer to serving.)
8. Open and pour in half and half and milk. Add butter and clams. Stir, garnish with reserved, cooked bacon, and serve.

Soups, Stews & Sauces

CREAM OF CHICKEN
WITH WILD RICE

Serves 4

Ingredients:

2	chicken breasts, boneless, skinless, diced medium
2T	butter
1c	onions, diced
1c	carrot, diced
1c	celery, diced
2	cans chicken stock
6oz	wild rice
1t	sea salt
½t	freshly ground black pepper
2T	water, 1T cornstarch (mixed)
4oz	cream cheese, cubed
1c	milk
1c	half and half

Instructions:

1. Set to "sear" and add butter. When melted, add onions, carrot, and celery and sauté.
2. Add chicken, cans of chicken stock, wild rice, sea salt, and fresh ground pepper.
3. Close lid and lock. Set to "soup" and adjust for 5 minutes.
4. When done, quick release until all pressure is released.
5. Open pressure cooker. Set to "slow cook" and simmer, adding cornstarch mixture in and stirring constantly.
6. Add cream cheese, stir until melted, and then pour in milk and half and half.
7. Pour or ladle into bowls and serve.

TURKEY SOUP
(FROM THANKSGIVING LEFTOVERS)

Serves 4

Ingredients:

- 2c   turkey, diced
- 1T   butter
- 1   onion, diced
- 4   carrots, peeled, cut into rounds
- 1   celery stalk, diced
- 6c   turkey stock
- 1t   sea salt
-     Egg noodles, cooked

Instructions:

1. Set to "sear" and add butter.
2. Once butter has melted, add onions and sauté for 1-2 minutes.
3. Add carrots and celery and sauté.
4. Add diced turkey and turkey stock.
5. Close lid and lock. Set to "soup" and adjust for 5 minutes.
6. When done, quick release until all pressure is released.
7. Open. Add sea salt and fresh ground pepper to taste.
8. Serve soup over cooked egg noodles.

Soups, Stews & Sauces

CREAMLESS CAULIFLOWER SOUP
WITH YUKON GOLD POTATOES

Serves 6

Ingredients:

- 2lbs cauliflower, cut into florets
- ¼lb peeled Yukon Gold potatoes
- 2½c milk
- 2 fresh bay leaves
- 2 sprigs of fresh thyme
- 1T sea salt
- Freshly ground white pepper

Instructions:

1. Place all ingredients in pressure cooker.
2. Close lid and lock. Set to "soup" and adjust for 10 minutes.
3. When done, quick release until all pressure is released.
4. Open. Remove bay leaves. With a slotted spoon, remove vegetables and place in a blender.
5. Add remaining milk/cooking liquid from cooker and ladle into the blender and cover with lid.
6. Blend the mixture to desired consistency. Serve.

Soups, Stews & Sauces

ITALIAN WEDDING SOUP
WITH BABY MEATBALLS

Serves 4

Ingredients:

- 1lb Italian sausage/ ground beef
- 1T olive oil
- 1 onion, diced
- 2 carrots, peeled, sliced thin
- 4c chicken stock
- 1 clove garlic
- ¼t sea salt
- ½t freshly ground black pepper
- 2c spinach
- 4T Parmesan cheese (garnish)
- 1c cooked fregola pasta or Israeli couscous

Instructions:

1. Roll Italian sausage into evenly sized meatballs.
2. Set cooker to "sear" and add oil, onions, and carrots. Sauté.
3. Add chicken stock, garlic, sea salt, and fresh ground pepper.
4. Add in meatballs.
5. Close lid and lock. Set to "soup" and adjust for 5 minutes.
6. When done, natural release for 35 minutes. Afterward, quick release until all pressure is released.
7. Open and add spinach. Stir well.
8. Garnish with Parmesan cheese. Serve hot.

Soups, Stews & Sauces

NACHO CHEESE SAUCE
FOR GAME DAY

Serves 4

Ingredients:

- 2T butter
- 2T flour
- 2c whole milk
- 6oz medium cheddar, shredded (about 1½c)
- ¼t sea salt
- ¼t chili powder
- 1 (5-oz) can diced tomatoes with green chilies

Instructions:

1. Set to "sear" and add butter and flour. Whisk together until mixture bubbles and becomes foamy.
2. Add milk, cheese, and diced tomatoes with green chilies.
3. Close lid and lock. Set to "soup" and adjust for 5 minutes.
4. When done, natural release, 5 minutes.
5. Afterward, quick release until all pressure is released.
6. Open and remove nacho cheese from pot. Stir in sea salt and chili powder to taste.

Tip: If sauce becomes too thick, whisk in an additional splash of milk.

Soups, Stews & Sauces

PORK POZOLE
WITH HOMINY

Serves 6

Ingredients:

- 1½lbs country-style ribs, pork butt, pork shoulder, diced into 1-inch cubes
- 2 (28-oz) cans of Mexican-style hominy (6c total cooked hominy)
- 1 (16-oz) jar salsa roja (or 2 indvl. 7-oz cans)
- 1 (15-oz) can or box chicken broth
- 1 head of garlic, cloves peeled
- 1T chicken base or pork/ham base
- 2T tequila or white wine (optional)
- 1t dried ground cumin (or ½ to 1t whole cumin seed, freshly ground)
- 1t dried ground coriander
- ½t freshly ground black pepper
- 1T vegetable oil

Instructions:

1. Using a colander, rinse canned hominy thoroughly with cold water.
2. Pat dry pork cubes.
3. Set to "sear" and add oil. Add pork (in batches) and sauté until browned, about 2 minutes.
4. Add 1c of the broth, chicken base or pork/ham base, tequila or white wine (optional), head of garlic, and salsa roja.
5. Close lid and lock. Set to "poultry" and adjust for 10 minutes.
6. When done, natural release for 35 minutes. Afterward, quick release until all pressure is released.
7. Open and add cumin and coriander. Stir.
8. Add fresh ground black pepper and sea salt to taste. Serve.

Soups, Stews & Sauces

CHICKEN SOUP
WITH FARRO & VEGETABLES

Serves 6

Ingredients:

- 4c chicken, diced, cooked
- 2T olive oil
- 1   onion, diced
- 3   carrots, peeled, diced
- 4   stalks celery, diced
- ¼c parsley, minced
- 1   bay leaf
- 4c water
- 1c farro, rinsed

Instructions:

1. Set to "sear" and add oil.
2. When oil is hot, add onions, carrots, and celery and sauté for 5 minutes.
3. Add cooked chicken, parsley, and water.
4. Add in farro.
5. Close lid and lock. Set to "soup" and adjust for 12 minutes.
6. When done, quick release until all pressure is released.
7. Open and remove bay leaf. Serve.

Soups, Stews & Sauces

BLACK BEAN SOUP
WITH COTIJA CHEESE

Serves 6

Ingredients:

- 1lb   dried black beans, rinsed thoroughly, soaked overnight
- 2T   extra-virgin olive oil
- 1   large white onion, diced fine
- 1   bell pepper, diced fine
- 5   cloves garlic, minced
- 1   bay leaf
- ½t   cumin
- ½t   oregano
- 1t   freshly ground black pepper
- 8c   water
- 2T   sherry vinegar
- ½c   dry white wine
- 1½t   salt

Garnish:

- 1   red bell pepper, diced
- 1   onion, diced
- 2   scallions, sliced
- 5oz   (half wheel) Cotija cheese, crumbled

Instructions:

1. In a large pan, heat oil and add onions, bell pepper, and garlic. Sauté until onions are soft, about 4-5 minutes.
2. Add bay leaf, cumin, oregano, and fresh ground black pepper and sauté for an additional 2 minutes.
3. In the pressure cooker, add ingredients from the pan. Add black beans and 8c water, sherry vinegar, wine, and salt.
4. Set to "soup" for 20 minutes.
5. When done, natural release for 35 minutes. Afterward, quick release until all pressure is released.
6. Open. Remove bay leaf and garnish with bell peppers, onions, and crumbled Cotija cheese.

Tip: Serve as a soup or over steamed rice.

Soups, Stews & Sauces

CARROT-GINGER SOUP

Serves 10

Ingredients:

- 6c carrots, sliced
- 10c vegetable stock
- 1t ground ginger or fresh ginger
- 2   cloves garlic, minced
- 6   green onions, thin slice
- 1c celery, small dice
- 1   large potato, peeled, diced
- 2c white or yellow onion, diced
- 1T olive oil
-     Sea salt and freshly ground black pepper to taste
- 1c half & half

Instructions:

1. Set to "sear" and add olive oil.
2. When oil is hot, add onions and sauté until translucent. Add garlic and celery and sauté for a couple of minutes.
3. Add potato, carrots, broth, and ginger, and add sea salt and fresh ground pepper to taste.
4. Close lid and lock. Set to "steam/veggies" and adjust for 8 minutes.
5. When done, quick release until all pressure is released.
6. Open and add half and half.
7. Blend the soup with an immersion blender or ladle into a countertop blender to mix.
8. Season with additional sea salt and ground black pepper to taste. Serve.

Soups, Stews & Sauces

MARINARA SAUCE (TRADITIONAL)

Serves 8

Ingredients:

- 2T   extra-virgin olive oil
- 4   onions, peeled, small dice
- 2-3   peppers, small dice
- 1-2   zucchini, small dice
- 2-4   stalks of celery, including leaves, chopped
- 3-4   large cans of whole, peeled tomatoes, chopped
- 1-2   cans of tomato paste
- 3   cloves of garlic, small dice
- 2   bay leaves
-      Oregano
-      Parsley
-      Dill

Instructions:

1. Set to "sear" and add oil. Add onions and sauté, stirring until onions are translucent, about 5-10 minutes.
2. Add in the remaining ingredients.
3. Close lid and lock. Set to "soup" and adjust for 15 minutes.
4. When done, natural release for 35 minutes. Afterward, quick release until all pressure is released.
5. Open and remove bay leaves. Using an immersion blender, blend the sauce.
6. Refrigerate, freeze, or serve.

Soups, Stews & Sauces

BLACK BEAN SOUP
WITH TOASTED CUMIN & CILANTRO

Serves 6

Ingredients:

- 1T olive oil
- 1c onions, small dice
- 1T mild or hot chili powder
- 1½t whole cumin seeds
- 1½t dried oregano leaves
- 7c water
- 1lb (2½c) dried black beans, picked over, rinsed
- 4oz Spanish chorizo, small dice
- 4 to 6 cloves garlic, minced
- 2 bay leaves
- Sea salt to taste

Avocado Salsa:

- 1 large, ripe Hass avocado, diced
- 2 large plum tomatoes, seeded, small dice
- ⅓c red onions, small dice
- ¼c cilantro, small dice
- 1 jalapeño (optional), seeded, diced
- 3T freshly squeezed lime juice
- Sea salt

Instructions:

1. Set to "sear" and add oil. When heated, add onions, chili powder, cumin seeds, and oregano. Sauté, stirring frequently until onions soften, about 1 minute.
2. Add water, beans, chorizo, garlic, and bay leaves.
3. Close lid and lock. Set to "beans" and adjust for 30 minutes.
4. When done, natural release for 35 minutes. Afterward, quick release until all pressure is released.
5. Open and stir well, remove bay leaves, and add sea salt to taste. Let the soup sit with no heat on; it will thicken.
6. Just before serving, in a bowl, prepare avocado salsa by tossing all ingredients together.
7. Ladle soup into bowls and top each portion with a large dollop of avocado salsa.

Soups, Stews & Sauces

MINESTRONE SOUP

Serves 4

Ingredients:

1T	extra-virgin olive oil
1	onion, small dice
2	carrots, diced
1	celery stalk, diced
1	zucchini, small dice
4	cloves garlic, minced
3lbs	tomatoes, peeled, seeded, and chopped
2	cans chicken stock
1lb	ditalini pasta
1t	Italian seasoning
1t	sea salt
½t	freshly ground black pepper
2c	baby spinach
1	can kidney beans
2T	basil, chopped
1c	Asiago cheese

Instructions:

1. Set to "sear" and add oil.
2. When oil is hot, add onions and sauté for 5 minutes.
3. Add garlic, carrots, celery, and zucchini and sauté.
4. Add tomatoes, chicken stock, pasta, and Italian seasoning.
5. Close lid and lock. Set to "soup" and adjust for 5 minutes.
6. When done, quick release until all pressure is released.
7. Open and add spinach, beans, and basil. Stir well to mix.
8. Pour into bowls and top with Asiago cheese. Serve.

Soups, Stews & Sauces

SPLIT PEA SOUP
WITH HAM

Serves 4

Ingredients:

- 3T unsalted butter
- 1 medium onion, finely diced
- 1 large rib celery, finely diced
- 1 (6-oz) ham steak, diced
- 2 medium cloves garlic, minced
- 1lb dried green split peas
- 6c low-sodium chicken stock
- 2 bay leaves
- Kosher salt and freshly ground black pepper

Instructions:

1. Set to "sear" and add butter.
2. Add onions, celery, and ham and sauté, stirring, until onions are soft but not browned, about 3 minutes.
3. Add garlic and cook until aromatic, about 30 seconds.
4. Add peas, chicken stock, and bay leaves. Stir to combine.
5. Close lid and lock. Set to "soup" and adjust for 20 minutes.
6. When done, quick release until all pressure is released.
7. Open, remove bay leaves, and stir soup until smooth. Season with salt and fresh ground pepper to taste. Serve.

Soups, Stews & Sauces

BORSCHT

Serves 2

Ingredients:

4	medium-sized beets, peeled, diced
3	carrots, peeled, shredded
2	red potatoes, cleaned, cut into cubes
1T	oil
1	onion, diced
1	can beef or chicken stock
2c	sauerkraut, drained, rinsed
3	cloves garlic, minced
1T	red wine vinegar
1T	sugar
	Freshly ground black pepper
	Sour cream (optional)

Instructions:

1. Place rack in bottom of pressure cooker and pour in 1½c of water.
2. Place beets on rack.
3. Close lid and lock. Set to "steam/veggies" and adjust for 30 minutes.
4. When done, quick release until all pressure is released.
5. Open and remove beets to a bowl; set aside. Remove rack.
6. Set cooker to "sear" and add oil. Add onions, and fresh ground pepper and sauté.
7. Return beets to cooker, and add carrots, potatoes, sauerkraut, and garlic.
8. Pour in can of beef or chicken stock, red wine vinegar, and sugar. Stir.
9. Close lid and lock. Set for 10 min.
10. When done, natural release for 35 minutes. Afterward, quick release until all pressure is released.
11. Open and ladle borscht into serving bowls. Top with sour cream (optional).

Soups, Stews & Sauces

BOURBON STREET GUMBO
WITH SHRIMP & ANDOUILLE

Serves 4

Ingredients:

- 2T extra-virgin olive oil
- 2T flour
- 12oz andouille sausage, sliced into ½-inch-thick coins
- 1 red bell pepper, small dice
- 2 ribs celery, small dice
- 1 yellow onion, small dice
- 2T Cajun or Creole seasoning
- 1 (14½-oz) can diced tomatoes, drained
- ⅔c chicken stock
- 2 bay leaves
- 1lb shrimp (peeled, optional)
  Sea salt
  Freshly ground black pepper
  Fresh parsley and/or chives
- 1 (10-oz) pkg. frozen okra
- 2T Worcestershire sauce

Instructions:

1. Set to "sear" and add olive oil and flour. Mix for a few minutes to make a brown roux.
2. When hot, add sausage and brown for 2-3 minutes per side.
3. Using a slotted spoon, remove sausage and transfer to a plate.
4. Add pepper, celery, onions, and Cajun seasoning and sauté for 1-2 minutes until very fragrant. Add okra.
5. Return sausage, and add tomatoes, chicken stock, Worcestershire sauce and bay leaves and stir.
6. Close lid and lock. Set to "fish" and adjust for 5 minutes.
7. When done, natural release for 35 minutes. Afterward, quick release until all pressure is released.
8. Open. Remove bay leaves. Set to "sear", add shrimp, and cook for 3-4 minutes. Shrimp should be opaque throughout when done.
9. Add sea salt and fresh ground black pepper to taste.
10. Top with parsley or chives. Serve with cooked rice.

Soups, Stews & Sauces

CHICKPEAS WITH TOMATOES

Serves 6

Ingredients:

- 3c chickpeas, rinsed, drained, and dried
- 8t olive oil
- 4t cumin seeds
- 1 large onion, thinly sliced
- 4t crushed garlic (extra, for more garlic flavor)
- 2t ground coriander
- 2t garam masala (add more for extra spice)
- 2t ground turmeric
- 2 (14-oz) cans diced tomatoes drained
- 3 large potatoes, peeled, cut into cubes
- ¼t sea salt
- ¼t freshly ground black pepper
- ½c water
- Fresh cilantro (garnish)

Instructions:

1. Add water (1 inch) on the bottom of pressure cooker, and add chickpeas. Close lid and lock. Set to "beans" and adjust for 10 minutes.
2. When done, quick release.
3. Open and remove chickpeas.
4. Set to "sear" and add oil.
5. When oil is hot, add cumin seeds and cook for approx. 30 seconds or until they start to crackle.
6. Add sliced onions and sauté for 5 minutes or until onions are golden and soft.
7. Stir in garlic, tomatoes, and other spices. Add remaining ingredients, except cilantro (for garnish) and return chickpeas to cooker.
8. Close lid and lock. Set for 15 minutes.
9. When done, natural release for 35 minutes. Afterward, quick release until all pressure is released.
10. Open and plate. Garnish with fresh cilantro and serve with basmati rice and warmed naan bread.

Soups, Stews & Sauces

TEXAS BEEF CHILI

Serves 4

Ingredients:

- 1lb grass-fed organic ground beef
- 1 green bell pepper, seeds removed, small dice
- 1 large onion, small dice
- 4 large carrots, small dice
- 1 (15-oz) can tomatoes, whole, drained, fine dice
- ½t freshly ground black pepper
- 1t sea salt
- 1t onion powder
- 1T chopped fresh parsley
- 1T Worcestershire sauce
- 4t chili powder
- 1t paprika
- 1t garlic powder
- Pinch of cumin

Garnish (optional):
Sour cream
Diced onions
Sliced jalapeños

Instructions:

1. Set to "sear" and add ground beef. Cook until brown and fat is rendered. Remove meat; discard fat.
2. Add in the remaining ingredients. Mix well.
3. Close lid and lock. Set to "meat/stew" and adjust for 35 minutes.
4. When done, natural release. Afterward, quick release until all pressure is released.
5. Open. Portion evenly and garnish with sour cream, diced onions, and jalapeños. Serve.

Soups, Stews & Sauces

POTATO LEEK SOUP

Serves 4

Ingredients:

- 8oz bacon, diced
- 1T   extra-virgin olive oil
- 3   large leeks, washed, sliced
- 1   onion, peeled, small dice
- 4   Yukon Gold potatoes
- 4c   chicken stock
- 1c   heavy cream
- 1T   dill, chopped
- 1T   parsley, chopped
-      Sea salt
-      Freshly ground black pepper

Instructions:

1. In a frying pan, cook bacon until done. Drain on paper towel; set aside.
2. Set cooker to "sear" and add oil.
3. Add leeks and onions and sauté for 4 minutes.
4. Add potatoes and chicken broth.
5. Close lid and lock. Set to "soup" and adjust for 5 minutes.
6. When done, quick release until all pressure is released.
7. Open and remove soup, pouring into a large bowl or saucepan to allow to slightly cool down.
8. Add cooked bacon, cream, and herbs to blender. Season with sea salt and freshly ground pepper.
9. Ladle into bowls and serve immediately.

Soups, Stews & Sauces

BEEF BURGUNDY
WITH ROOT VEGETABLES & RED WINE

Serves 4

Ingredients:

- 1½lbs lean boneless beef chuck roast, cut into 1-inch pieces
- 2 medium carrots, peeled, large dice
- 2 medium parsnips, peeled, large dice
- 4 Yukon Gold potatoes, cubed
- 2⅔c (8oz) fresh mushrooms, halved
- ¾c onions, cut into wedges
- 2 garlic cloves, minced
- 1 bay leaf
- ¾t sea salt
- ½t dried thyme, crushed
- ¼t freshly ground black pepper
- ⅔c beef broth or beef stock
- ⅔c dry red wine
- 2T tomato paste
- 2T flour
- ¼c water
- 6c cooked egg noodles (or 12oz uncooked)

Instructions:

1. In cooker, combine beef, carrots, mushrooms, onions, parsnips, garlic, bay leaf, sea salt, thyme, fresh ground black pepper, beef stock or broth, red wine, and tomato paste.
2. Close lid and lock. Set to "soup" and adjust for 12 minutes.
3. When done, natural release for 35 minutes. Afterward, quick release until all pressure is released.
4. Open and remove the bay leaf.
5. In a small bowl, add flour and ¼c water. Combine. Mix well.
6. Add mixture to pressure cooker.
7. Set to "sear" and adjust for 8 minutes (do not replace lid). Cook until stew has thickened and is bubbling, stirring frequently.
8. Serve Beef Burgundy over cooked egg noodles.

Soups, Stews & Sauces

CHICKEN & DUMPLING SOUP

Serves 4

Ingredients:

- 2 chicken breasts, boneless, cut into halves
- 7c chicken stock
- 2 stalks of celery
- ½ onion, large dice
- Sea salt
- Freshly ground black pepper

Dumplings:

- 3c flour
- 1T baking powder
- 1¼t sea salt
- 1c milk

Instructions:

1. Set to "sear" and place chicken pieces, stock, celery, and onions in cooker.
2. Cook chicken through and soften onions.
3. In a bowl, prep dumplings by mixing flour, baking powder, sea salt, and milk.
4. Place dough on a floured surface or cutting board. Using a pizza cutter, cut the dough into cubes.
5. Add dough to cooker.
6. Close lid and lock. Set to "steam/veggies" and adjust for 3 minutes.
7. When done, natural release for 35 minutes. Afterward, quick release until all pressure is released.
8. Open and remove chicken pieces only. Allow meat to slightly cool. Chop up chicken.
9. Return chicken pieces to cooker. Stir and serve.

Soups, Stews & Sauces

BUTTERNUT SQUASH SOUP

Serves 6

Ingredients:

1½lbs butternut squash, peeled, cubed
3T butter
½c green onions, diced
½c celery, diced
½c carrots, diced
1 clove of garlic, minced
2 (14½-oz) cans chicken broth
⅛t dry red pepper flakes
¼t freshly ground black pepper
⅛t ground nutmeg

Instructions:

1. Set to "sear" and add butter.
2. When butter has melted, add onions, celery, and carrots and sauté.
3. Add butternut squash, garlic, and chicken stock. Add red pepper flakes, fresh ground pepper, and nutmeg.
4. Close lid and lock. Set to "steam/veggies" and adjust for 10 minutes.
5. When done, quick release until all pressure is released.
6. Open. Using an immersion blender, blend the contents or pour contents into blender and blend well.
7. Pour soup into bowls and serve immediately.

Soups, Stews & Sauces

HOMEMADE VEGETABLE SOUP

Serves 6

Ingredients:

    Extra-virgin olive oil
1   small onion, small dice
3   carrots, peeled, small dice
3   celery stalks, small dice
10 green beans, cut into 1-inch pieces
¼   head green cabbage, small dice
2   potatoes, small dice
¼c barley
1T parsley, fine chop
2   sprigs thyme
1   bay leaf
1t   oregano
4c chicken or beef stock
1   (24-oz) can, whole, peeled tomatoes, roughly chopped
    Sea salt and freshly ground black pepper to taste

Instructions:

1. Set to "sear" and add oil, carrots, and celery.
2. Add onions and sauté for 1 minute.
3. Add in the rest of the ingredients.
4. Close lid and lock. Set to "soup" and adjust for 25 minutes.
5. When done, natural release for 35 minutes. Afterward, quick release until all pressure is released.
6. Open and remove bay leaf and sprigs. Add sea salt and fresh ground pepper to taste. Stir soup and serve.

LENTIL SOUP

Serves 4

Ingredients:

1	medium potato, peeled, small dice
2	medium carrots, small dice
1c	lentils
1c	stock
5c	water
1	bay leaf
½t	smoked paprika or Hungarian paprika
	Fresh rosemary
1T	olive oil (for dry sauté, no oil)
1	small onion, minced
1	clove garlic, minced

After cooking:
Sea salt and freshly ground pepper to taste.

Instructions:

1. Set to "sear" and add oil.
2. When hot, add onions and sauté until translucent.
3. Add garlic and sauté for 1 or 2 additional minutes.
4. Add in lentils and all remaining ingredients for the soup.
5. Close lid and lock. Set to "soup" and adjust for 10 minutes.
6. When done, natural release for 35 minutes. Afterward, quick release until all pressure is released.
7. Add sea salt and fresh ground pepper to taste. Serve.

Soups, Stews & Sauces

PHO GA

Serves 4

Ingredients:

2T	extra-virgin olive oil
2	yellow onions, halved
1T	ginger, sliced
1	small bunch cilantro
2	star anise
1	cinnamon stick
4	whole cloves
1t	fennel seed
1t	coriander seeds
6	chicken drumsticks
¼c	fish sauce
2T	sugar

For Serving:

4	servings pho noodles
1	yellow onion, sliced thin
⅓c	scallions, sliced
2c	trimmed bean sprouts
1	lime, cut into wedges
	Hoisin or Sriracha sauce

Instructions:

1. Set to "sear" and add oil.
2. Add onions and ginger and cook for 5 minutes.
3. Add in cilantro, star anise, cinnamon, cloves, fennel, coriander, and chicken drumsticks.
4. Pour in 2 quarts of water, and add fish sauce and sugar.
5. Close lid and lock. Set to "poultry" and adjust for 20 minutes.
6. When done, quick release until all pressure is released.
7. Open and remove chicken legs. Strain broth into a bowl, removing any solids.
8. Season broth to taste with more fish sauce and sugar, if needed.
9. Place noodles in bowl, pour hot broth over noodles.
10. Add a chicken leg, and garnish with bean sprouts, onions, scallions, and your choice of hoisin or Sriracha sauce.

Soups, Stews & Sauces

CORN & MUSHROOM SOUP

Serves 4

Ingredients:

1T	extra-virgin olive oil
1	onion, small dice
2	carrots, peeled, small dice
2	stalks celery, small dice
1	pkg. mushrooms, small dice
2	cloves garlic, minced
2	cans chicken stock
½t	dried thyme
1t	sea salt
½t	freshly ground black pepper
	Dash red pepper flakes
4c	potatoes, peeled, cut into cubes
2c	half and half
4c	corn kernels, fresh or frozen

Instructions:

1. Set to "sear" and add oil.
2. When oil is hot, add carrots, celery, and onions and sauté.
3. Add mushrooms and garlic.
4. Add 1 can of the chicken stock, thyme, sea salt, freshly ground pepper, red pepper flakes. Add cubed potatoes and corn.
5. Close lid and lock. Set to "soup" and adjust for 4 minutes.
6. When done, natural release for 35 minutes. Afterward, quick release until all pressure is released.
7. Set cooker to "slow cook" and simmer soup, then puree with extra stock. Gradually stir in remaining can of chicken stock. Stir in half and half to soup.
8. Pour soup into bowls and serve.

Soups, Stews & Sauces

CHICKEN TORTILLA SOUP

Serves 6

Ingredients:

1½lbs chicken breasts
6c   chicken stock
⅓c   flour
2T   tomato paste
2T   paprika
2t   chili powder
1t   garlic powder
1T   cumin
1t   cayenne
3T   taco seasoning
1   onion, diced
1   can black or pinto beans, rinsed

Garnish (optional):

     Sour cream
1   avocado, cubed
1   lime, cut into wedges
1   lime, (juice only)
     Tortilla strips

Instructions:

1. In a bowl, add flour, tomato paste, and spices and whisk in 1c of the chicken stock.
2. Add remaining stock to pressure cooker.
3. Add the chicken, onions, and beans.
4. Close lid and lock. Set to "soup" and adjust for 10 minutes.
5. When done, quick release until all pressure is released.
6. Open and carefully remove chicken. Transfer to a plate.
7. Shred the chicken with forks. Return meat to cooker and into liquid.
8. Pour into bowls and top with tortilla strips. Garnish (optional) with sour cream, cubed avocado, and lime wedges. Serve.

Soups, Stews & Sauces

SOUP OF THE SEVEN SEAS

Serves 6

Ingredients:

- 2lbs whitefish (tilapia, grouper, or snapper), cut into 2-inch pieces
- 1lb shrimp, peeled, deveined
- 4oz mussels, shelled
- 4oz calamari, sliced
- 8oz octopus tentacles, cut into bite-sized pieces
- 4 small blue crab, cut, quartered including shell
- 1c onions, diced
- 1c green bell peppers, diced
- 1c fresh epazote*
- 2c diced tomato
- 2T lime juice
- 1t sea salt
- 8c fish stock or chicken broth cilantro, lime, and hot sauce (served on side)

Instructions:

1. Set to "sear" and add onions, peppers, and epazote. Sauté for 3 minutes.
2. Add whitefish and cook for an additional 2 minutes.
3. Add calamari, shrimp, mussels, octopus, and crab.
4. Add lime juice, stock, and tomatoes. Close lid and lock. Set to "soup" and adjust for 12 minutes.
5. When done, natural release for 35 minutes. Afterward, quick release until all pressure is released.
6. Serve in bowl and add your toppings. Serve cilantro, lime, and hot sauce on the side.

*Disclaimer: Women who are pregnant or nursing should not consume epazote. Small children should not consume epazote.

Soups, Stews & Sauces

TOMATO BASIL BISQUE
WITH HERB CROUTONS

Serves 4

Ingredients:

- 2T   extra-virgin olive oil
- 5   carrots, peeled, small dice
- 1   large yellow onion, small dice
- 1T   dried basil
- 3   cans (28oz each) whole Italian-style tomatoes
- 1   (14½-oz) can low-sodium chicken broth
- 1c   heavy (whipping) cream
-      Kosher salt
-      Freshly ground black pepper

Garnish:

- 2T   lightly packed fresh basil leaves, cut into fine ribbons
-      Herb croutons

Instructions:

1. Set to "sear" and add olive oil.
2. When hot, add onions, basil, and carrots and sauté for 5 minutes.
3. Add cans of tomatoes, low-sodium chicken broth, salt, and fresh ground black pepper.
4. Close lid and lock. Set to "soup" and adjust for 40 minutes.
5. When done, natural release for 35 minutes. Afterward, quick release until all pressure is released.
6. Open. Using an immersion blender, blend soup until smooth.
7. Add heavy whipping cream and stir to combine.
8. Pour into bowls, top with basil ribbons and herb croutons, and serve.

Soups, Stews & Sauces

DITALINI SOUP

Serves 4

Ingredients:

16oz ditalini pasta
1 zucchini, medium size, diced
1 yellow squash, medium size, diced
1 red onion, medium size, diced
1 fresh corn cob, kernels cut off
2c fresh kale, rinsed, stems removed, chopped small
1 fresh large tomato, diced
1 small shallot, diced
3 cloves garlic, minced
1 sprig of rosemary, finely chopped
2T extra-virgin olive oil
4c chicken or vegetable stock
Sea salt
Freshly ground black pepper

Instructions:

1. Add oil and set to "sear".
2. Add shallots, red onion, garlic, rosemary, and ¼t of freshly ground black pepper. Stir and cook for 2 to 3 minutes or until onions soften.
3. Add zucchini, yellow squash, tomato, corn kernels, and kale. Stir and then add pasta and chicken stock.
4. Close lid and lock. Set to "soup" and adjust for 8 minutes.
5. When done, quick release until all pressure is released.
6. Open. Season to taste with sea salt and fresh ground black pepper.

Soups, Stews & Sauces

TOM KA GAI

Serves 4

Ingredients:

- 2 (14-oz) cans coconut milk
- 2c water
- ¾lb shredded chicken, boiled or roasted
- 1T fresh ginger, peeled, julienned
- 1T extra-virgin olive oil
- 2T Sriracha sauce
- 2T fish sauce
- 2 (3-inch-long) pieces lemon grass
- ½ red onion, small size, julienned
- ½t turmeric
- ¼t cayenne pepper
- 1 kaffir or bay leaf, fresh (preferred) or dried
- 1 lime, zest and juice
- ¼c cilantro leaves, chopped (for garnish)
- 2 green onions, sliced thin (for garnish)
- Sea salt
- Freshly ground black pepper

Instructions:

1. Set to "sear" and add olive oil. Add onions, turmeric, cayenne pepper, kaffir or bay leaf. Cook 2 to 3 minutes or until fragrant. Spices will lightly brown.
2. Flatten out lemon grass using a rolling pin or pan. Chop up fine and add to cooker.
3. Add ginger, garlic, fish sauce, and Sriracha. Pour in coconut milk and water. Add chicken.
4. Close lid and lock. Set to "soup" and adjust for 7 minutes.
5. When done, quick release until all pressure is released.
6. Open and stir. Season to taste, if necessary, and add sea salt and fresh ground pepper. Add lime zest and juice. Stir to combine.
7. Garnish soup with cilantro and green onions.

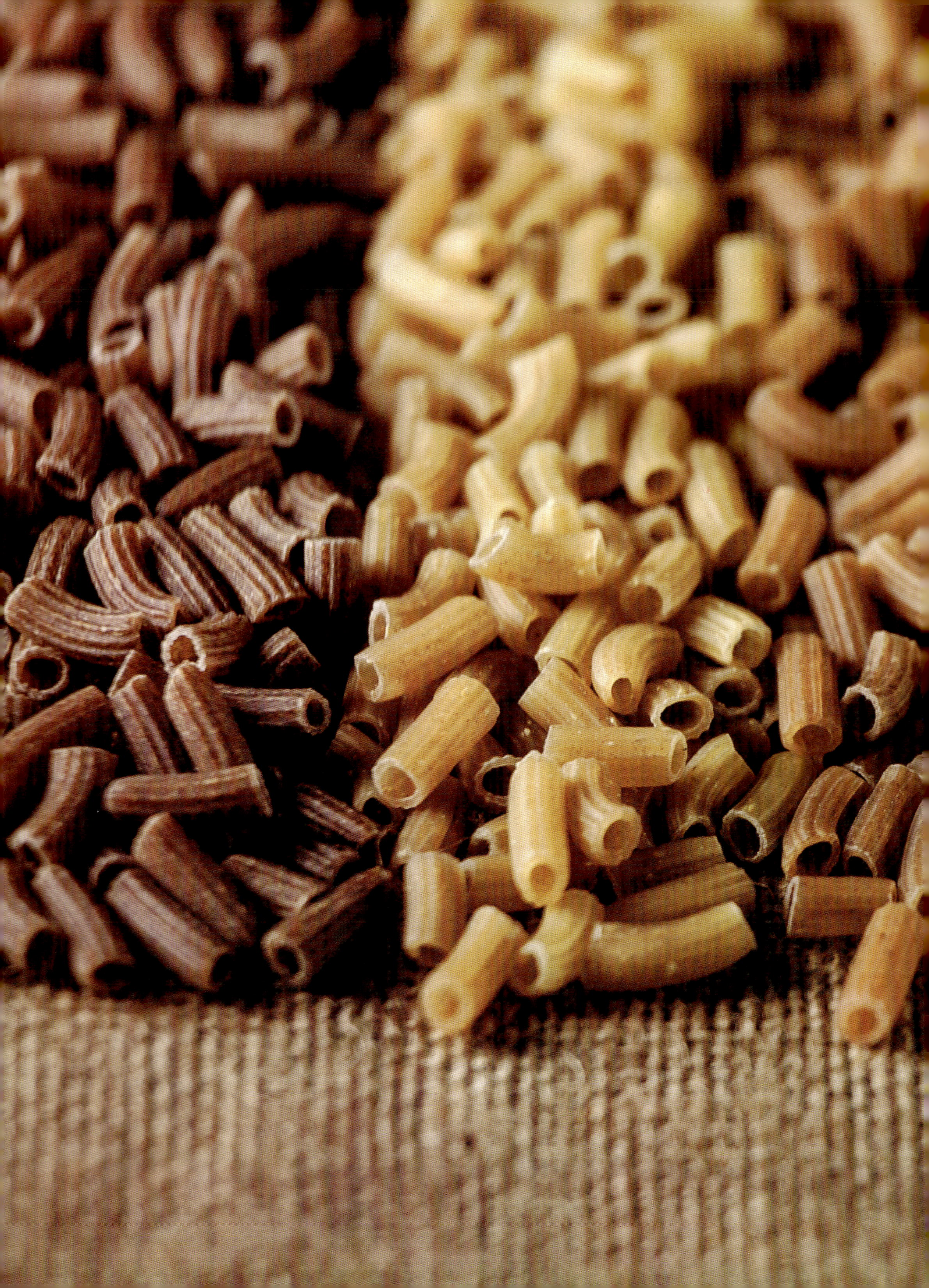

RICE, GRAINS & PASTAS

Basmati Rice with Lemongrass 58	**Kale Risotto** 79
Black Beans with Chorizo 59	**Rigatoni Bolognese** 81
Arroz con Pollo (Rice with Chicken) 61	**Orzo Pasta with Slow-Cooked Lamb** 82
Black-Eyed Peas & Rice 62	**Polenta with Mascarpone** 83
Chickpea Hummus 63	**Mushroom Risotto** 85
7-Bean Chili 65	**Refried Beans** 87
Bulgur Wheat Pilaf 66	**Red Beans and Rice** 89
Israeli Couscous with Diced Vegetables & Curry 67	**Sesame-Ginger Rice with Broccoli** 91
Ditalini with Zucchini & Tomatoes 69	**Ziti with Sausage Ragu** 93
Dirty Rice 70	**Vegetarian Green Pozole** 94
Creamy Chicken Penne 71	**Wild Rice from Minnesota** 95
Cuban Rice 73	**Spicy Indian Dal** 97
Farro 74	**Mac & Cheese** 98
Couscous 75	**Wild Rice with Pecans & Chives** 99
Hoppin' John 77	
Jasmine Rice with Sesame Seeds 78	

Rice, Grains & Pastas

BASMATI RICE
WITH LEMONGRASS

Serves 2

Ingredients:

- 1c   basmati rice
- 2   lemongrass stalks, cut into pieces
- 2c   water
- Sea salt to taste
- Few drops sesame oil

Instructions:

1. Soak rice in water for 15-20 minutes. Drain; set aside.
2. Put rice and lemongrass into pressure cooker and then add water, sea salt, and sesame oil.
3. Close lid and lock. Set to "rice" and adjust for 4 minutes.
4. When done, natural release for 35 minutes. Afterward, quick release until all pressure is released.
5. Open and remove from pot, discard stalks, and fluff with fork.
6. Add few drops sesame oil and add sea salt to taste.

Rice, Grains & Pastas

BLACK BEANS
WITH CHORIZO

Serves 4

Ingredients:

- 1lb   dried black beans
- 6oz   Spanish-style chorizo, cut into ¼-inch half moons
- 3   whole cloves of garlic
- 2   bay leaves
- 2qt   chicken stock
- 2t   sea salt
- 2   chipotle chilies in adobo sauce
- 1   onion, chopped in half
- Cilantro for garnish

Instructions:

1. Set to "sear" and add the chorizo. Cook until fats are released and meat starts to crisp.
2. Add beans, onion halves, garlic, bay leaves, chipotle chilies with adobo sauce, sea salt, and chicken stock.
3. Close lid and lock. Set to "beans" and adjust for 40 minutes.
4. When done, natural release for 35 minutes. Afterward, quick release until all pressure is released.
5. Open and discard onion halves and bay leaf. Season with sea salt, garnish with cilantro, and serve.

Rice, Grains & Pastas

ARROZ CON POLLO
(RICE WITH CHICKEN)

Serves 6

Ingredients:

2lbs chicken thighs, boneless, skinless, cut into quarters
1½c uncooked long-grain white rice
½c pimientos, sliced (for garnish)
½c sweet peas, drained, (for garnish)
1t saffron threads
3T warm water
1t sea salt
5 cloves of garlic, minced
¼c vegetable oil
½ red bell pepper, diced
1 medium Spanish onion, diced
½t ground cumin
1t dried oregano
2c chicken broth

Instructions:

1. In a bowl, place saffron threads in warm water; set aside.
2. Clean and pat dry chicken and place in a separate bowl. Add sea salt and garlic. Set chicken in refrigerator for 30 minutes.
3. When ready to cook, set to "sear" and add oil.
4. Place chicken in pressure cooker and brown, cooking in batches, if necessary.
5. Add diced bell peppers and onions. Sauté for 3 minutes.
6. Add cumin, oregano, chicken stock, rice, and saffron water. Stir to combine.
7. Bring up to a boil and cook for 5 minutes.
8. Close lid and lock. Set to "rice" and adjust for 17 minutes.
9. When done, natural release for 35 minutes. Afterward, quick release until all pressure is released.
10. Open and fluff rice with a fork. Serve on a large platter and garnish with sliced pimientos and sweet peas.

Rice, Grains & Pastas

BLACK-EYED PEAS & RICE

Serves 4

Ingredients:

- 2c basmati rice
- 1 can black-eyed peas, drained, liquid reserved
- Water, as needed
- 1 can coconut milk
- ½t allspice
- ½t dried thyme
- ¼t salt
- ¼t garlic powder
- ¼t black pepper
- 2 green onions, thinly sliced, white parts, couple inches of green parts
- 3 plum tomatoes cut into quarters

Instructions:

1. Pour reserved liquid from black-eyed peas and coconut milk into a large measuring cup. Add enough water to make a total of 3½c liquid.
2. Pour rice, liquid, peas, and place rest of ingredients into pressure cooker.
3. Close lid and lock. Set to "rice" and adjust for 8 minutes.
4. When done, natural release for 10 minutes.
5. Afterward, quick release until all pressure is released.
6. Open. Let stand for 2 minutes.
7. Fluff with fork and serve.

Rice, Grains & Pastas

CHICKPEA HUMMUS

Serves 4

Ingredients:

- 1c   dry chickpeas, soaked overnight
- 1   bay leaf
- 3-4   cloves garlic, crushed
- 2T   (heaping) of tahini paste
- 1   lemon, (juice only)
- ¼t   cumin powder
- ½t   sea salt
- ½   bunch parsley, chopped (about ¼c of leaves)
- Paprika
- Extra-virgin olive oil

Instructions:

1. Drain chickpeas and place in pressure cooker. Cover with 6c of water. Add 1-2 crushed garlic cloves and bay leaf.
2. Close lid and lock. Set to "beans" and adjust for 18 minutes.
3. When done, natural release for 35 minutes. Afterward, quick release until all pressure is released.
4. Open and drain chickpeas; reserve all of the liquid.
5. When cooled, pick out bay leaf and pour chickpeas into a food processor.
6. Add ½c of reserved cooking liquid and tahini paste, lemon juice, cumin, and 1-2 fresh garlic cloves.
7. Puree, slowly incorporating additional reserved cooking liquid to reach desired consistency. Hummus should be creamy without being runny.
8. Add sea salt to taste. Mix well.
9. Garnish with paprika and fresh parsley and serve.

Rice, Grains & Pastas

7-BEAN CHILI

Serves 4

Ingredients:

Beans:
- 1 (20-oz) bag bean mix
- 2qts water

Chili:
- 2T vegetable oil
- 1 large jalapeño, minced
- 3 cloves garlic, minced
- 1 onion, diced
- ½t kosher salt
- ¼c chili powder
- 2T ground cumin
- 1T ground coriander
- 1t dried oregano
- ¼t cocoa powder (optional)
- ⅛t ground cloves (optional)
- 1t kosher salt
- 6c water
- 1 (15-oz) can fire-roasted, crushed tomatoes
- 1t freshly ground black pepper
- Kosher salt to taste (2t more kosher salt, optional)
- Lime wedges for serving

Instructions:

1. Rinse beans and place in a large container. Cover with 2qts of water. Soak beans for at least 8 hours, or overnight.
2. When ready to cook, set to "sear" and add oil.
3. Add onions, jalapeño, garlic, and ½t of the salt. Sauté until onions are soft and brown around the edges, about 8 minutes.
4. Stir in chili powder, cumin, coriander, oregano, cocoa powder, and cloves. Toast for 1 minute.
5. Drain and rinse beans. Pour into pressure cooker. Add ½t of the kosher salt. Stir to coat.
6. Add 6c of water and tomatoes.
7. Close lid and lock. Set to "beans" and adjust for 18 minutes.
8. When done, natural release for 35 minutes. Afterward, quick release until all pressure is released.
9. Remove and puree 2c of the beans and liquid (use 4c from a wet measuring cup; use immersion blender).
10. Stir puree back into cooker, adding in the fresh ground black pepper. Add kosher salt to taste and serve with lime wedges.

Rice, Grains & Pastas

BULGUR WHEAT PILAF

Serves 4

Ingredients:

- ½c   bulgur wheat
- ¾c   water
- 1   medium onion, diced
- 1   1-inch piece of ginger, fresh, minced
- 3   cloves garlic, minced
- 1   carrot, medium dice (optional)
- ½c   bell pepper, medium dice (optional)
- 2T   coriander leaves, finely chopped (optional)
- ¼t   chili powder (optional)
-       Sea salt to taste
- 1T   vegetable oil
- 1   cinnamon stick (1 inch)
- 1T   parsley (for garnish)

Instructions:

1. In a saucepan, add water and bring up to a boil. Add pinch of sea salt.
2. Place bulgur wheat in a bowl. Add boiled, salted water to the bulgur. Cover and let sit for 10-15 minutes.
3. Set pressure cooker to "sear" and add oil.
4. Add cinnamon and garlic and sauté for a few seconds, and then add onions, and ginger. Sauté until onions are transparent.
5. Add bell pepper and carrots (substitute vegetables with broccoli, corn, cauliflower, or peas).
6. Add chili powder, and sea salt, to taste, if needed. Pour reserved bulgur wheat from bowl into cooker.
7. Close lid and lock. Set to "rice" and adjust for 4 minutes.
8. When done, natural release for 35 minutes. Afterward, quick release until all pressure is released.
9. Open and fluff with a fork.

Rice, Grains & Pastas

ISRAELI COUSCOUS
WITH DICED VEGETABLES & CURRY

Serves 4

Ingredients:

- 1T olive oil
- 2 bay leaves
- ½ onion, small dice
- 1 red bell pepper, cored, seeded, medium dice (optional)
- 1c grated carrot (optional)
- 1¾c couscous
- 1¾c water
- 2t sea salt to taste
- 1T curry
- ½t garam masala
- 1T lemon juice
- Cilantro to garnish

Instructions:

1. Set to "sear" and add olive oil.
2. Add bay leaves and onions, and sauté for 2 min.
3. Add bell peppers and carrots, and sauté for 1 additional minute (if using).
4. Add couscous, water, garam masala, sea salt, and curry. Stir well.
5. Close lid and lock. Set to "rice" and adjust for 2 minutes.
6. When done, natural release, 10 minutes.
7. Afterward, quick release until all pressure is released.
8. Open. Fluff couscous with fork, add lemon juice and garnish with cilantro. Serve.

Rice, Grains & Pastas

DITALINI
WITH ZUCCHINI & TOMATOES

Serves 6

Ingredients:

- 1 (16-oz) bag dry cannellini beans
- 1 zucchini, cut into half moons
- 1 onion, small dice
- 1lb ground turkey
- 8c chicken broth
- 28oz diced tomatoes
- 1 clove garlic, minced
- 1c white wine
- 1lb ditalini pasta
- Romano cheese, for garnish

Instructions:

1. Clean, rinse, and dry the beans.
2. Place beans in pressure cooker with 2c chicken broth, onions, and garlic.
3. Close lid and lock. Set to "beans" and adjust for 15 minutes.
4. When done, quick release until all pressure is released.
5. Open and remove beans; set aside.
6. Set cooker to "sear" and add ground turkey. Cook, stirring to crumble until fully done, approximately 5 minutes.
7. Add rest of chicken broth, tomatoes, and white wine. Pour in beans.
8. Close lid and lock. Set for 30 minutes.
9. When done, quick release until all pressure is released.
10. Open and add pasta and zucchini.
11. Close lid and lock. Set to "potatoes" and adjust for 4 minutes.
12. When done, quick release until all pressure is released.
13. Open and garnish with Romano cheese and serve.

Rice, Grains & Pastas

DIRTY RICE

Serves 4

Ingredients:

½lb chicken livers, chopped
3oz bacon, chopped
5oz long-grain rice
2c vegetable stock
1 large onion, chopped
2 celery stalks, chopped
2 garlic cloves, minced
1 sprig parsley, chopped
½t paprika
½t oregano
½t thyme
½t salt
¼t cayenne pepper
¼t freshly ground black pepper
1T olive oil

Instructions:

1. Set to "sear" and add olive oil.
2. When oil is hot, add onions and sauté until almost soft, about 3 minutes.
3. Add celery and bacon and sauté for an additional 3 minutes, stirring occasionally.
4. Add all spices, garlic, chicken livers, and rice. Mix well.
5. Add the stock, using it to help scrape up the bits stuck to bottom of cooker.
6. Close lid and lock. Set to "rice" and adjust for 4 minutes.
7. When done, natural release for 35 minutes. Afterward, quick release until all pressure is released. Open. Fluff rice with a fork and garnish with parsley. Serve.

Rice, Grains & Pastas

CREAMY CHICKEN PENNE

Serves 4

Ingredients:

- 1lb chicken breasts, cubed
- 2c   penne pasta
- 1c   water (or 1 can chicken stock)
- 1T   basil
- 1t   oregano
- 2   cloves garlic, chopped
- 1   onion, diced
- ¼t   red pepper flakes
-      Sea salt and fresh ground pepper to taste
- 2oz cream cheese
- ½c   Parmesan cheese
-      Mushrooms (optional)

Instructions:

1. Add all ingredients, except cream cheese and Parmesan.
2. Push pasta down so it is submerged in liquid.
3. Close lid and lock. Set to "rice" and adjust for 7 minutes.
4. When done, natural release, 5 minutes. Afterward, quick release until all pressure is released.
5. Open and add Parmesan and cream cheese. Stir until the cream cheese is melted and incorporated.
6. Top with parsley and additional Parmesan cheese.

Rice, Grains & Pastas

CUBAN RICE

Serves 4

Ingredients:

- 3T warm water with 1t saffron
- 2lbs boneless, skinless chicken thighs, cut into quarters
- 2t sea salt
- 5 cloves garlic, minced
- ¼c vegetable oil
- ½ red bell pepper, small dice
- 1 medium Spanish onion, small dice
- ½t ground cumin
- 1t dried oregano
- 2c chicken broth
- 1½c uncooked long-grain white rice
- ½c sliced pimientos or smoked piquillo peppers (for garnish)
- ½c sweet peas, strained (for garnish)

Instructions:

1. Clean and dry chicken. Rub chicken all over with sea salt and minced garlic.
2. Set to "sear" and add oil.
3. When oil is hot, add chicken and brown, stirring occasionally, for 3 minutes.
4. Add bell pepper and onions. Sauté for an additional 3 minutes.
5. Add cumin, oregano, chicken stock, rice, and saffron mixture. Stir to combine.
6. Bring up to a boil and cook for 5 minutes.
7. Close lid and lock. Set to "rice" and adjust for 17 minutes.
8. When done, natural release for 35 minutes. Afterward, quick release until all pressure is released.
9. Open and fluff rice with fork. Garnish with sliced pimientos or piquillo peppers and sweet peas.

Rice, Grains & Pastas

FARRO

Serves 4

Ingredients:

- 2c farro, rinsed
- 2c water
- Seasoning of choice

Instructions:

1. Add water, farro, and seasonings to pressure cooker.
2. Close lid and lock. Set to "rice" and adjust for 13 min. Press "start."
3. When done, natural release, 5 minutes.
4. Afterward, quick release until all pressure is released.
5. Open. Drain any remaining liquid and serve.

Rice, Grains & Pastas

COUSCOUS

Serves 4

Ingredients:

2T butter
2½c chicken broth
1 (16-oz) pkg. Israeli couscous
Sea Salt and freshly ground pepper to taste
Cucumber (optional)
Tomato (optional)

Instructions:

1. Set to "sear" and add butter. When melted, add broth and couscous. Stir to combine.
2. Close lid and lock. Set to "time" and adjust for 3 minutes.
3. When done, quick release until all pressure is released.
4. Open and fluff couscous with a fork.
5. Add sea salt and fresh ground pepper to taste and serve.

Rice, Grains & Pastas

HOPPIN' JOHN

Serves 6

Ingredients:

- 2c   black-eyed peas
- 2c   long-grain rice
- 1   small onion, finely diced
- 1   red bell pepper, diced
- 8oz smoked bacon, diced, fat rendered
- 1T   Cajun seasoning
- 4c   water (for the beans)
- 2c   water (to cook rice)

Instructions:

1. Place long-grain rice and 2c water in pressure cooker.
2. Close lid and lock. Set to "rice" for 10 minutes.
3. When done, quick release until all pressure is released.
4. Open and remove cooked rice.
5. Set to "sear" and add smoked bacon, cooking until crispy.
6. Remove bacon and leave in the fat.
7. To the fat, add all vegetables and sweat them; do not brown.
8. Add black-eyed peas, cover with water, and add Cajun seasoning.
9. Close lid and lock. Set to "beans" and adjust for 30 minutes.
10. When done, quick release until all pressure is released.
11. Open and check to see if peas and vegetables are cooked. If not, close lid and set for an additional 15 minutes.
12. When done, serve over prepared rice.

Rice, Grains & Pastas

JASMINE RICE
WITH SESAME SEEDS

Serves 2

Ingredients:

- 1c jasmine rice
- 1T Asian sesame oil
- 1t unsalted butter
  Kosher salt, to taste
- 1T black sesame seeds, toasted (optional)
- 1t white sesame seeds, toasted (optional)
- 1½c water

Instructions:

1. Rinse rice; drain.
2. Pour rice in cooker along with butter, water, and oil. Close lid and lock.
3. Set cooker to "rice" and adjust for 10 minutes.
4. When done, quick release until all pressure is released.
5. Open, fluff with fork. Add in sesame seeds.

Rice, Grains & Pastas

KALE RISOTTO

Serves 4

Ingredients:

- 2T oil
- 1c onions, chopped
- 2 cloves garlic, minced
- 1½c Arborio rice
- ½c white wine
- 3½c vegetable stock
- 1 bunch of kale (2c), finely chopped
- ½t sea salt
- ¼t pepper flakes
- ½c Parmesan cheese

Instructions:

1. Set to "sear" and add oil.
2. When oil is hot, add onions and garlic and sauté.
3. Add rice. Pour in wine and stir for 1 minute. Pour in vegetable stock.
4. Close lid and lock. Set to "rice" and adjust for 4 minutes.
5. When done, quick release until all pressure is released.
6. Open. Place kale in and cook, stirring constantly for about 5 minutes.
7. Stir in cheese and add pepper flakes. Serve.

Rice, Grains & Pastas

RIGATONI BOLOGNESE

Serves 6

Ingredients:

- 4oz pancetta, or bacon (unsmoked), cubed
- 1 medium onion, finely diced
- 1 medium carrot, finely diced
- 1 medium celery stalk, finely diced
- 2lbs ground beef
- ½c dry white wine
- 5T tomato paste concentrate
- 1c beef stock
- 1T sea salt
- ¼t pepper
- 2 (24-oz cans) crushed tomatoes
- Rigatoni pasta, cooked

Instructions:

1. Place pancetta in the bottom of pressure cooker, laid flat in a single layer.
2. Set to "slow cook" to render fat.
3. After pancetta begins to slightly sizzle, or after 5 minutes, add onions, carrot, and celery.
4. Cook until well softened, about 10 minutes. Add small amount of butter or olive oil if ingredients begin to stick.
5. Set cooker to "sear" and add ground beef. Brown well, stirring occasionally, about 5-7 minutes.
6. Add wine, scrape bits from bottom and sides of pan, and cook until wine has evaporated, about 7 minutes.
7. In a medium bowl, mix tomato paste with beef stock, sea salt, and pepper. Pour stock mixture into the cooker and stir well.
8. Close lid and lock. Set to "rice" for 10 minutes.
9. When done, quick release until all pressure is released.
10. Open and add 1½c water and stir well, scraping bottom and sides.
11. Close lid and lock. Set for an additional 10 minutes.
12. When done, quick release until all pressure is released.
13. Open. Serve bolognese over cooked rigatoni.

Rice, Grains & Pastas

ORZO PASTA
WITH SLOW-COOKED LAMB

Serves 4

Ingredients:

1½-lb leg of lamb, 1-inch dice
2T extra-virgin olive oil
½t kosher salt
½t black pepper
4 cloves garlic, minced
2½c orzo pasta, cooked
1c water
2 (28-oz) cans crushed tomatoes
1pt grape tomatoes, cut in half
⅓c Kalamata olives, chopped
4oz feta crumbles
½ red onion, cut into thin strips
¼c pine nuts
5oz baby spinach

Instructions:

1. Set to "sear" and adjust for 2 minutes and add olive oil.
2. When oil is hot, add salt, fresh ground pepper, pine nuts, and garlic and sauté, stirring continuously.
3. Add lamb and sauté for 5 minutes. Cook until thoroughly browned. Remove cooked lamb from pot; set aside. Add orzo.
4. Close lid and lock. Set to "rice" and adjust for 9 minutes.
5. When done, quick release until all pressure is released.
6. Open and drain remaining liquid; remove pasta to platter.
7. Add lamb mixture and spinach to cooker and sauté for 30 seconds to wilt spinach. Remove lamb and spinach.
8. Combine lamb mixture with the pasta. Add tomatoes, olives, and cheese. Mix and serve immediately.

Rice, Grains & Pastas

POLENTA
WITH MASCARPONE

Serves 4

Ingredients:

- 2c   cornmeal (polenta)
- 2½c water
- 1t   sea salt
- 1t   freshly ground black pepper
- ¼c   mascarpone cheese
- 2T   grated Parmesan cheese
- 2T   butter

Instructions:

1. Place water, polenta, butter, and sea salt in pressure cooker. Stir to combine.
2. Close lid and lock. Set to "rice" and adjust for 7 minutes.
3. When done, natural release for 35 minutes. Afterward, quick release until all pressure is released.
4. Open, add mascarpone cheese, and stir until smooth. Add sea salt and fresh ground pepper to taste.
5. Top with grated Parmesan cheese and serve.

Tip: Polenta will thicken as it cools. For a thicker consistency, cook until desired consistency is reached.

Rice, Grains & Pastas

MUSHROOM RISOTTO

Serves 4

Ingredients:

- 1qt   chicken or vegetable stock
- 1oz   dried porcini mushrooms
- 1½lbs mixed mushrooms, trimmed, sliced thin, stems reserved
- 4T   extra-virgin olive oil
- 4T   unsalted butter
-       Kosher salt and freshly ground black pepper
- 1   medium yellow onion, finely chopped
- 2   medium cloves garlic, finely minced
- 1½c risotto rice (Arborio)
- 1t   Worcestershire sauce
- ¾c   dry white wine
- ¼c   heavy cream
- 1oz   Parmigiano-Reggiano cheese, grated fine, plus more for serving
-       Handful finely minced mixed herbs: parsley, chervil, tarragon, and/or chives

Instructions:

1. Pour chicken or vegetable stock and dried mushrooms in a microwave-safe bowl. Set in the microwave on high for 5 minutes.
2. Remove mushrooms from stock. Give mushrooms a rough chop. Reserve the stock left in the bowl.
3. In the pressure cooker, set to "sear" and adjust for 8 minutes.
4. Add olive oil and fresh mushrooms, season with salt and fresh ground pepper. Stir occasionally and cook until mushrooms are browned.
5. Add onions, garlic, and porcini mushrooms and cook, stirring frequently until onions are soft, about 4 minutes.
6. Add rice and stir until rice is evenly coated with oil and toasted but not browned, about 3-4 min.
7. Add wine and cook until the alcohol has evaporated, about 2 min.
8. Pour stock from microwave-safe bowl into the pressure cooker pot. Add Worcestershire sauce. Ensure all ingredients are submerged in cooker.
9. Close lid and lock. Set to "steam/veggies" for 5 minutes.
10. When done, quick release until all pressure is released.
11. Open and stir to combine any remaining liquid.
12. Stir in heavy cream, cheese, butter and herbs. If risotto is too soupy, cook a few minutes longer. If it's too thick, add a little hot water.
13. Season to taste with salt and fresh ground pepper, sprinkle with freshly grated cheese, and serve.

Rice, Grains & Pastas

REFRIED BEANS

Serves 6

Ingredients:

- 1T olive oil
- 1 jalapeño, cored, seeded, and finely chopped
- 1 small onion, chopped (½c)
- 3-4 cloves garlic, finely minced
- 1½lbs dry pinto beans, rinsed
- 8c water
- 4c chicken or vegetable broth
- 2t sea salt
- 2T white vinegar

Instructions:

1. Set to "sear" and add oil, jalapeño, onions, and garlic. Sauté for 1-2 minutes, stirring often.
2. Add beans, water, broth, sea salt, and vinegar.
3. Close lid and lock. Set to "multi grain" and adjust for 35 minutes.
4. When done, natural release for 35 minutes. Afterward, quick release until all pressure is released.
5. Open. Reserve 2 cups of the liquid in a separate bowl. Drain the rest of liquid.
6. Using an immersion blender or potato masher, process/mash beans to desired consistency, adding reserved cooking water as needed to achieve desired consistency.
7. Serve, refrigerate, or freeze.

Rice, Grains & Pastas

RED BEANS & RICE

Serves 4

Ingredients:

- 3T olive oil or vegetable oil
- 1lb ground smoked sausage, preferably andouille, sliced into ½-inch-thick rounds
- 2 medium onions, small dice
- 7 cloves garlic, minced
- 1T Creole seasoning
- Sea salt
- Freshly ground black pepper
- 1 medium rib celery, diced
- 1 medium green bell pepper, diced
- 1T dried basil
- 3 bay leaves
- 1lb dried red beans
- 1 scallions, thinly sliced
- 2T hot sauce (of choice) (garnish)
- Cooked rice (to serve with)

Instructions:

1. Set to "sear" and add oil. When oil is hot, add sausage and brown, stirring frequently. Remove to paper towel-lined plate. Leave the grease in the pot.
2. Add onions and sauté for 5 minutes, or until tender, add Creole seasoning, sea salt, and fresh ground pepper.
3. Add garlic and cook for 2-3 minutes.
4. Add celery and bell pepper. Cook until celery is translucent.
5. Add beans, bay leaves, and enough water to cover.
6. Return sausage to cooker and stir.
7. Close lid and lock. Set to "multi grain" and adjust for 35 minutes.
8. Cook rice separately according to package instructions.
9. When done, natural release for 35 minutes. Afterward, quick release until all pressure is released.
10. Open and check to see if beans are tender. If underdone, set for an additional 3 minutes, and then natural release for 35 minutes, quick release until all presure is released. Repeat, if necessary.
11. When beans are tender, stir in scallions. Reserve some scallions for garnish.
12. Serve over rice.

Rice, Grains & Pastas

SESAME-GINGER RICE
WITH BROCCOLI

Serves 2

Ingredients:

- 1c rice
- 2c water
- 1lb broccoli florets, blanched
- ½c chopped red bell pepper
- ¼c sliced slivered almonds
- ⅓c seasoned rice vinegar
- 2T soy sauce
- 1T sesame oil
- 2T water
- 2T ginger, minced
- 1   clove garlic, minced
- ⅛t (pinch) red pepper flakes

Instructions:

1. Combine rice, water, and sesame oil in pressure cooker.
2. Close lid and lock. Set to "rice" and adjust for 4 minutes.
3. When done, natural release for 35 minutes. Afterward, quick release until all pressure is released.
4. Open and add chopped red pepper, almonds, and broccoli.
5. In a small bowl, combine remaining ingredients and pour over rice mixture. Toss to combine.

Rice, Grains & Pastas

ZITI
WITH SAUSAGE RAGU

Serves 6

Ingredients:

2T	olive oil	½t	dried crushed red pepper
4oz	thinly sliced pancetta, diced	2c	dry red wine
2lbs	pork shoulder, cut into 1¼-inch cubes	1	(28-oz) can plum tomatoes in juice, tomatoes chopped, juice reserved
1lb	Italian hot sausages, casings removed	1¼lbs	ziti pasta, cooked
2c	chopped onions	2c	coarsely packed, grated whole-milk mozzarella
¾c	chopped carrots		
¾c	chopped celery	½c	Parmesan cheese, freshly grated
6	large fresh thyme sprigs		Sea salt
6	large garlic cloves, chopped		Freshly ground black pepper
2	bay leaves		

Instructions:

1. Set to "sear" and add pancetta. Sauté until golden brown, about 6 minutes.
2. Remove pancetta and transfer to a bowl, leaving drippings in cooker.
3. Sprinkle sea salt on pork shoulder cubes and add freshly ground black pepper. Add 1c of the red wine to drippings.
4. Place pork shoulder cubes in cooker and sauté until brown, about 7 minutes.
5. Remove and transfer all pork to the bowl with pancetta.
6. Add Italian sausage to cooker and sauté until no longer pink, while breaking up meat, about 5 minutes.
7. Add onions, carrots, celery, thyme, garlic, bay leaves, and crushed red pepper. Sauté until vegetables are tender, about 10 minutes.
8. Add wine. Bring up to a boil, scraping up any browned bits. Return pancetta and pork, with any accumulated juices, to cooker. Bring up to a boil and cook for 2 minutes.
9. Add tomatoes with juice.
10. Close lid and lock. Set to "poultry" and adjust for 13 minutes.
11. When done, quick release until all pressure is released.
12. Open. Transfer to large bowl or platter. Mix in mozzarella and Parmesan until cheese is evenly distributed and thoroughly melted. Serve with pasta. Remove bay leaves before serving.

Rice, Grains & Pastas

VEGETARIAN GREEN POZOLE

Serves 6

Ingredients:

- 2 (28-oz) cans of Mexican-style hominy
- 16oz salsa verde
- 15oz vegetable broth (or other, non-meat-based broth)
- 1 head garlic
- 1t ground cumin
- 1t ground coriander
- ½t freshly ground black pepper
- Sea salt
- 2t tequila (optional)

Instructions:

1. Rinse hominy in cold water.
2. Add broth, garlic, hominy, salsa verde, and tequila (optional) to cooker.
3. Close lid and lock. Set to "soup" and adjust for 10 minutes.
4. When done, quick release until all pressure is released.
5. Open and add cumin, coriander, and fresh ground pepper. Stir.
6. Add sea salt to taste, if needed. Ladle pozole into bowls, garnish, and serve.

Rice, Grains & Pastas

WILD RICE
FROM MINNESOTA

Serves 4

Ingredients:

- 1⅔T canola oil
- 1 yellow onion, diced
- 2c sliced mushrooms
- 2 cloves garlic, finely minced
- 2c wild rice and brown rice medley, rinsed, drained
- 2½c vegetable stock
- ¼c freshly chopped parsley
- Sea salt and freshly ground pepper to taste

Instructions:

1. Set to "sear" and add oil.
2. When hot, add onions and mushrooms and sauté for about 4 minutes, stirring frequently.
3. Add garlic and sauté for an additional 30 seconds.
4. Add rice to toast, cooking 2-3 minutes, stirring constantly.
5. Turn off heat, add vegetable stock, and scrape to remove any rice stuck to the sides and the bottom.
6. Close lid and lock. Set to "multi grain" and adjust for 20 minutes.
7. When done, natural release for 35 minutes. Afterward, quick release until all pressure is released.
8. Open and fluff rice with fork.
9. Add sea salt and fresh ground pepper to taste. Garnish with parsley, and serve.

Rice, Grains & Pastas

SPICY INDIAN DAL

Serves 4

Ingredients:

- 1   2-inch piece of ginger, peeled, finely chopped
- 6   garlic cloves
- 1   large onion, finely chopped
- 1-2T canola oil
- 1t   black mustard seeds
- 3   small, dried red chilies, split
- 1t   coriander seeds
- 1t   cumin seeds
- ½t   fenugreek
- 2c   chana dal, yellow lentils rinsed thoroughly and sorted
- 6c   vegetable broth
- 1½t sea salt
- 1t   garam masala
- 1t   turmeric
- 5oz   fresh baby spinach, rinsed, drained well

Garnishes:

Plain Greek yogurt
Cilantro, chopped

Instructions:

1. Add ginger, garlic, and onion to a food processor. Pulse until mixture is pureed.
2. Set cooker to "sear" and add oil. When oil is hot, add in onion mixture, black mustard seeds, and red chili pieces. Sauté until the seeds begin to pop.
3. Grind coriander seeds, cumin seeds, and fenugreek together in a spice grinder.
4. Add to pot and sauté 1-2 additional minutes.
5. Add chana dal, broth, sea salt, garam masala, and turmeric.
6. Close lid and lock. Set to "potato" and adjust for 5 minutes.
7. When done, natural release for 35 minutes. Afterward, quick release until all pressure is released.
8. Open. Add spinach and stir to combine.
9. Serve over cooked basmati rice and garnish with a dollop of Greek yogurt. Sprinkle chopped cilantro on top.

Rice, Grains & Pastas

MAC & CHEESE

Serves 8

Ingredients:

- 3c dry elbow pasta
- 3c water
- 1   (14½-oz) can evaporated milk
- 4oz cream cheese
- 1T butter
- 4c grated Parmesan cheese
- 4c sharp cheddar cheese (or smoked Gouda)
- ½t dry mustard powder
- ½t onion powder
- ½t freshly ground black pepper
- 1t sea salt
- 2T cornstarch

Instructions:

1. Pour water into pressure cooker. Place dry pasta in.
2. Close lid and lock. Set to "multi grain" and adjust for 5 minutes.
3. When done, quick release until all pressure is released.
4. Open and stir pasta to separate noodles.
5. In a small bowl, mix evaporated milk, cornstarch, onion powder, mustard powder, sea salt, and fresh ground black pepper.
6. Add mixture into pasta in the cooker. Add Parmesan cheese, cheddar or smoked Gouda, butter, and cream cheese.
7. Set to "sear" and cook until sauce thickens, 5 to 6 minutes.

Rice, Grains & Pastas

WILD RICE
WITH PECANS & CHIVES

Serves 4

Ingredients:

- 2c wild rice
- 6c water
- 1t sea salt
- ½c chopped or whole pecans
- 1T apple cider vinegar
- 1T fresh chopped chives
- 1 Granny Smith apple, cored, diced
- 2T hazelnut oil
- ½c chives

Instructions:

1. Combine rice, water, and salt in pressure cooker. Add vinegar.
2. Close lid and lock. Set to "rice" and adjust for 25 minutes.
3. When done, natural release for 35 minutes. Afterward, quick release until all pressure is released.
4. Open and fluff rice with fork.
5. Fold in pecans. Add chives and Granny Smith apples. Finish with hazelnut oil.

MEATS

Balsamic Chicken Thighs	102
Barbacoa Beef	103
Asian Braised Pork with Chilies & Ginger	105
BBQ-Style Tri-Tip Beef	106
Brisket	107
Beef Cheeks with Carrots	109
Beef Stroganoff with Egg Noodles	110
Beef Tips with Onions & Mushrooms	111
Braised Chicken with White Wine & Olives	113
British Pot Roast	114
Butter-Braised Turkey Breast	115
Chicken Alfredo	117
Chicken Burrito Bowls	118
Chicken Fajitas	119
Braised Lamb Shanks with Root Vegetables	121
Chicken Adobo	122
Braised Turkey Thighs with Yukon Gold Potatoes & Cranberries	123
Beef Osso Buco with Gremolata	125
Chicken Pot Pie	126
Chicken Puttanesca	127
Chorizo & Chicken with Cuban Rice	129
Chicken Tikka Masala	130
Chicken Tinga from Mexico	131
Chicken Cacciatore (Hunter Style)	133
Chicken with Coconut Curry	134
Chicken with Italian Seasoning	135
Chicken Mole	137
Corned Beef & Cabbage	138
Easter Ham	139
Cider-Braised Pork Stew	141
Indian Butter Chicken	142
Italian Beef	143
Cuban Ropa Vieja	145
Jamaican-Style Oxtail	146
Green Chili Pork Stew	147

- Green Chili Pulled Pork Carnitas 149
- Kalua Pig 150
- Lemon-Butter Chicken with Fresh Herbs 151
- Korean Short Ribs 152
- My Mom's Meatloaf.................. 154
- Navarin of Lamb 155
- Kung Pao Chicken..................... 157
- Orange Chicken 158
- Picadillo... 159
- Stuffed Flank Steak 160
- Pork Belly (with Chinese Spices)........................ 161
- Lengua (Beef Tongue) in Salsa Verde 163
- Sausage and Peppers 164
- Pulled Pork Carnitas 165
- Yankee Pot Roast with Mushrooms 167
- Pork Shanks with Beer & Fennel Seeds................ 169
- Slow-Cooked Buffalo Chicken Wings.......................... 171
- Slow-Braised Brisket with BBQ Sauce........................ 172
- Southern-Style Smothered Chicken.................. 173
- Pork Chops in Buttermilk Sauce 175
- Sugo Maille (Braised Pork Sauce) 176
- Tri-Tip Beef in Mushroom Red Wine Sauce 177
- Stout Beer BBQ Ribs................ 179
- Turkey Osso Buco with Onions & Tomatoes 180
- Veal Blanquette........................ 181
- Swedish Meatballs in Gravy 183
- Veal Osso Buco 184
- Whole Braised Chicken with Sriracha............................ 185
- Yankee Pot Roast with Cider ... 186
- Chicken Breasts in Balsamic-Dijon Sauce............................... 187

Meats

BALSAMIC CHICKEN THIGHS

Serves 4

Ingredients:

- 8 chicken thighs, skinless
- ¼t sea salt
- ¼t freshly ground black pepper
- 2t olive oil
- ¼c shallots, minced
- 1T fresh thyme, minced
- ¼c dry red wine
- ¼c balsamic vinegar
- ¼c chicken broth
- ¼c honey
- 1 bay leaf

Instructions:

1. Set to "sear" and add oil.
2. Season chicken thighs with sea salt and fresh ground black pepper.
3. Place chicken in and sear until golden brown on each side, about 3-5 minutes; set aside.
4. Add shallots and thyme and sauté until soft and shallots are golden.
5. Pour wine into cooker and deglaze the bottom to release the bits. When most of the liquid has evaporated, add balsamic vinegar, chicken broth, honey, and bay leaf.
6. Return chicken to cooker.
7. Close lid and lock. Set to "poultry" and adjust for 5 minutes.
8. When done, quick release until all pressure is released.
9. Open and remove bay leaf. Serve.

Meats

BARBACOA BEEF

Serves 4

Ingredients:

2½lbs chuck roast, cut into 3 pieces
1   onion, quartered
3T apple cider vinegar
¼c lime juice
6   cloves garlic
3   dried chipotle peppers
1c beef stock
2t ground cumin
1T dried oregano
½t ground cloves
1T tomato paste
    Sea salt and freshly ground black pepper
1T oil
2   bay leaves

Instructions:

1. Add onions, vinegar, lime juice, garlic, chipotle, beef stock, cumin, oregano, cloves, and tomato paste to blender. Blend until smooth.
2. Season beef with salt and pepper.
3. Set to "sear" and add oil.
4. When oil is hot, add meat and sear for 7 minutes.
5. Add bay leaves and sauce.
6. Close lid and lock. Set to "meat/stew" and adjust for 60 minutes.
7. When done, natural release for 35 minutes. Afterward, quick release until all pressure is released.
8. Open and remove bay leaves.
9. Remove beef and transfer to plate. Shred beef with fork and let sit for 10 minutes to absorb juices.

Tip: Serve "as is" or as tacos, burritos, or in nachos.

Meats

ASIAN BRAISED PORK
WITH CHILIES & GINGER

Serves 6

Ingredients:

3lbs pork shoulder, boneless, trimmed, cut into 2-inch-thick strips
4 whole dried ancho chilies, seeds and stems removed
2 whole dried pasilla chilies, seeds and stems removed
32oz can low-sodium chicken stock
½c raisins
1c frozen orange juice concentrate
1 can chipotle chilies canned in adobo
2T white vinegar
2T Asian fish sauce
2T vegetable oil
2 medium onions, sliced thin
6 medium garlic cloves, minced
2t dried oregano
1T ground cumin
3 bay leaves
 Kosher salt
 Cilantro, diced, onions, lime wedges (all optional)

Instructions:

1. Set to "sear" and add dried chilies. Sauté, stirring frequently until slightly darkened, or 2-5 minutes.
2. Add chicken stock, raisins, orange juice concentrate, chipotles in adobo, white vinegar, and fish sauce.
3. Bring up to a boil, and then reduce to a simmer, cooking until chilies are soft, about 15 minutes.
4. Using a stick blender, blend until smooth and pureed; set aside.
5. Pat dry the pork.
6. Set to "sear" and add oil. Heat until smoking.
7. Add pork and brown on all sides, about 8 min. Remove pork; set aside.
8. Add onions and garlic. Sauté, stirring frequently until onions and garlic are soft and are beginning to brown, about 10 minutes.
9. Add oregano and cumin, stirring constantly, about 30 seconds.
10. Add pureed chili mixture to cooker. Stir and scrape up any browned bits from the bottom.
11. Dice pork into 2-inch chunks and return meat to cooker. Add bay leaves.
12. Bring up to a boil and then reduce heat to a simmer, stirring occasionally.
13. Cover with glass lid. Set to "slow cook" and adjust for 2 hours.
14. When done, pork will break apart with a spoon and sauce will be thick. Season with salt to taste. Remove bay leaves.
15. Serve pork with corn tortillas, cilantro, diced onions, lime wedges, and queso fresco cheese (optional).

Meats

BBQ-STYLE TRI-TIP BEEF

Serves 4

Ingredients:

- 1 tri-tip roast
- 2 carrots, peeled, chopped
- 1 onion, chopped
- 1lb mushrooms, whole, cleaned, and quartered
- 1-2 cloves of garlic, peeled, minced
- ¼c butter
- 1c BBQ sauce of your choice
- Sea salt
- Freshly ground black pepper
- ½c water

Instructions:

1. Season roast with sea salt and fresh ground black pepper.
2. Set to "sear" and add meat. Sear meat on each side. Remove meat; set aside.
3. Place carrots, onions, mushrooms, garlic, and butter in cooker and sauté.
4. Return beef to cooker and add BBQ sauce and water.
5. Close lid and lock. Set to "meat/stew" and adjust for 17 minutes (for medium-rare).
6. When done, quick release until all pressure is released.
7. Open and serve.

Meats

BRISKET

Serves 4

Ingredients:

- 3lbs flat cut beef brisket
- 2T Worcestershire sauce
- 1c water
- 1T celery salt
- ½c brown sugar
- 2T apple cider vinegar
- 1t sea salt
- Freshly ground black pepper
- 1t garlic salt
- ½t onion powder

Instructions:

1. In a large bowl or resealable plastic bag, combine all ingredients including brisket and marinate overnight.
2. When ready to cook, place marinated beef brisket in pressure cooker. Add all remaining marinade to pot.
3. Close lid and lock. Set to "meat/stew" and adjust for 60 minutes.
4. When done, natural release for 35 minutes. Afterward, quick release until all pressure is released.

Tip: Remove brisket to cutting board and allow meat to rest for several minutes. Then, slice against the grain.

Meats

BEEF CHEEKS WITH CARROTS

Serves 4

Ingredients:

2¼lbs beef cheeks, chopped
12 pearl onions, peeled, root ends intact
1   large onion, finely diced
5T olive oil, divided
2T flour
1   dried bay leaf
1   sprig fresh thyme
2   sprigs flat-leaf parsley
3   garlic cloves, crushed
½c dry red wine
¼c water
3   carrots, chopped
1½T balsamic vinegar glaze
    Sea salt and freshly ground black pepper to taste
    Parsley, extra, chopped (for garnish)

Instructions:

1. Set to "sear" and add 2T of the olive oil. Add pearl onions and sauté until they are light brown, about 5 minutes. Remove onions; set aside.
2. In a large bowl, season flour. Add beef, toss to coat, and shake off excess.
3. Heat 1T of the olive oil in pressure cooker. Cook beef in batches until browned. Remove; set aside.
4. Tie bay leaf, parsley, and thyme together with kitchen string (bouquet garni).
5. Heat remaining oil. Return onions to cooker and add garlic. Sauté until onions and garlic are tender.
6. Return beef to cooker and add wine, water, and bouquet garni.
7. Close lid and lock. Set to "meat/stew" and adjust for 20 minutes.
8. When done, quick release until all pressure is released.
9. Open and add onions and carrots.
10. Close lid and lock. Set for 5 minutes.
11. When done, quick release until all pressure is released.
12. Open and add balsamic vinegar glaze. Stir. Season with sea salt and fresh ground black pepper to taste. Garnish with chopped parsley.

Meats

BEEF STROGANOFF
WITH EGG NOODLES

Serves 6

Ingredients:

1½lbs beef chuck, cut into 1-inch pieces
Kosher salt
Freshly ground black pepper
1T olive oil
1 medium onion, chopped
1c dry white wine
1t Dijon mustard
1T all-purpose flour
1c low-sodium beef broth
1lb whole white button mushrooms
3 carrots, cut into ½-inch chunks
2 celery stalks, chopped
¼c Neufchatel cheese
¼c roughly chopped fresh parsley
12oz whole wheat egg noodles, cooked

Instructions:

1. Toss beef with ½t of salt and ½t fresh ground pepper.
2. Set to "sear" and add oil.
3. Add beef and brown on all sides, about 4 min.
4. Add onions, stirring frequently until onions soften and begin to brown, about 4 minutes.
5. Add white wine, mustard, and flour. Bring to a simmer and cook until liquid is reduced by half, about 2 minutes.
6. Add beef broth, mushrooms, carrots, and celery.
7. Close lid and lock. Set to "meat/stew" and adjust for 18 minutes.
8. When done, quick release until all pressure is released.
9. Open and stir in Neufchatel cheese and add parsley. Add salt and fresh ground pepper to taste.
10. Serve over cooked egg noodles, prepared according to package.

Meats

BEEF TIPS
WITH ONIONS & MUSHROOMS

Serves 6

Ingredients:

5-6lbs	sirloin tip or chuck roast, trimmed, cut into bite-sized pieces
2	onions, chopped
3	garlic cloves, minced
8oz	mushrooms, sliced
2	(32-oz) cans or boxes beef broth
	Green onions for garnish
	Sea salt
	Freshly ground black pepper
1T	Worcestershire sauce
2T	olive oil

Instructions:

1. Add oil to pressure cooker and set to sear. Add onions and garlic and sauté. When almost done, add mushrooms and continue to sauté until cooked.
2. Remove onions, garlic, and mushrooms; set aside.
3. Drain off any liquid cooked out of mushrooms, and add more oil. Heat until oil is almost smoking.
4. Season meat well with sea salt and fresh ground pepper.
5. Add meat to skillet in small amounts and brown. Remove meat; place in a bowl. Repeat until all are cooked.
6. Add one can (or box) of beef broth.
7. Transfer meat to pressure cooker and pour in additional can (or box) of broth.
8. Close lid and lock. Set to "meat/stew" and adjust for 12 minutes.
9. When done, quick release until all pressure is released.
10. Serve with buttered noodles.

Meats

BRAISED CHICKEN
WITH WHITE WINE & OLIVES

Serves 4

Ingredients:

- 1 whole chicken, cut into parts, or package of bone-in chicken pieces, skin removed
- ½c dry white wine
- 3½oz salt-cured olives (Taggiasca, French, or Kalamata), rough chop
- 1 fresh lemon, sliced, for garnish (optional)

Marinade:

- 2 garlic cloves, finely chopped
- 3 sprigs fresh rosemary, finely chopped
- 2 sprigs fresh sage, finely chopped
- ½ bunch parsley leaves (with stems)
- 3 lemons, juice only (about ¾c)
- 4T extra-virgin olive oil
- 1t sea salt
- ¼t freshly ground black pepper
- 1½c water

Instructions:

1. For the marinade, place garlic, rosemary, sage, and parsley in a container and add lemon juice, olive oil, sea salt, and fresh ground black pepper. Mix well.
2. Place chicken in a deep dish. Cover well with ¾ of the marinade; reserve ¼ of the marinade. Cover with plastic wrap and marinate in refrigerator for 2-4 hours.
3. When ready to cook, set pressure cooker to "sear" and add olive oil.
4. Add chicken and brown the pieces on all sides (without lid on) for about 5 minutes; remove chicken and set aside.
5. Deglaze the bottom of cooker with white wine until liquid has almost completely evaporated, about 3 minutes.
6. Return chicken to pressure cooker, dark meat first, with breasts on top.
7. Add the 1½c water to the ¼ reserved marinade (makes 1½c liquid). Pour marinade on top of chicken.
8. Close lid and lock. Set to "poultry" and adjust for 10 minutes.
9. When done, quick release until all pressure is released.
10. Open. Remove chicken and place on a serving platter. Cover with foil.
11. With the lid off, set to "sear" and reduce cooking liquid by ¼ until thick and syrupy.
12. Set to "slow cook" and return chicken to pressure cooker.
13. Mix chicken in with the glaze reduction and simmer for a few minutes.
14. Remove braised chicken and sprinkle with rosemary, olives, and lemon slices. Serve.

BRITISH POT ROAST

Serves 6

Ingredients:

- 3 lbs boneless beef chuck roast, trimmed
- 2T vegetable oil
- Freshly ground black pepper
- Pinch seasoned salt, to taste
- Pinch onion powder, to taste
- 14½oz beef broth
- 1½T Worcestershire sauce
- 1 large onion, cut into 4 wedges
- 4 carrots, peeled, cut into bite-sized pieces
- 4 large potatoes, peeled, cut into bite-sized pieces

Instructions:

1. Set to "sear" and add oil.
2. Add beef and brown the roast on all sides. Season with fresh ground pepper, seasoned salt, and onion powder.
3. Pour in beef broth and Worcestershire sauce, and add quartered onions.
4. Close lid and lock. Set to "meat/stew" and adjust for 30 minutes.
5. When done, quick release until all pressure is released.
6. Open and add carrots and potatoes.
7. Close lid and lock. Set for an additional 15 minutes.
8. When done, quick release until all pressure is released.
9. Open. Remove roast and vegetables to serving dish.

Meats

BUTTER-BRAISED TURKEY BREAST

Serves 4

Ingredients:

1   (6-lb) turkey breast, bone-in, skin on
14oz chicken or turkey broth
1   large onion, quartered
1   celery stalk, cut into large pieces
1   sprig of thyme
3T cornstarch
3T cold water
6T butter
Sea salt and freshly ground black pepper

Instructions:

1. Heavily season turkey breast with sea salt and fresh ground black pepper.
2. In the pressure cooker, set to "sear" and add butter, onions, celery, and thyme. Sauté until golden brown.
3. Place cooking rack into cooker pot, add broth, then lay turkey on rack breast down.
4. Close lid and lock. Set to "poultry" and adjust for 30 minutes.
5. When done, quick release until all pressure is released.
6. Open cooker and insert meat thermometer into the thickest part of the breast; the temperature should read "165°F" or higher. If it reads below this temperature, close the lid and lock and cook for an additional 15 minutes. Afterward, quick release until all pressure is released, then check once again with thermometer.
7. Once the turkey is done, remove the breast and place on a platter, cover with foil, and allow to rest.
8. Skim the fat off the liquid remaining in the pressure cooker (use ladle or remove pot and carefully pour and skim, or use a fat separator). Pour into a bowl.
9. Add cold water with cornstarch. Mix well. Pour back into the cooker (will help thicken broth and make it into a gravy). Season with sea salt and fresh ground pepper to taste, if needed.

Meats

CHICKEN ALFREDO

Serves 4

Ingredients:

- 2 chicken breasts, diced
- 2c water
- 8oz dry fettuccine pasta
- 2T olive oil
- Sea salt
- 2T freshly ground black pepper

Alfredo Sauce:
- 1c heavy cream
- ¼c butter
- 1½c grated Parmesan
- ¼c parsley, chopped

Instructions:

1. Set to "sear" and add olive oil.
2. Season chicken with sea salt and fresh ground black pepper. When oil is hot, add chicken and sear on both sides until golden brown.
3. Add water and pasta (break pasta into halves or thirds).
4. Close lid and lock. Set to "multi grain" and adjust for 3 minutes.
5. When done, quick release until all pressure is released.
6. Open and add Alfredo sauce. Stir well. Add sea salt and fresh ground pepper to taste.
7. Top with Parmesan cheese and parsley and serve.

Meats

CHICKEN BURRITO BOWLS

Serves 4

Ingredients:

- 1½lbs chicken thighs, boneless, skinless
- 1T olive oil
- 1 small onion, diced
- 1 clove garlic, minced
- 1t chili powder
- ½t sea salt
- 1 can black beans, rinsed
- 1c white rice
- 1c salsa
- 2c chicken broth
- ¼c cilantro
- ¼c cheddar cheese

Instructions:

1. Set to "sear" and add oil and chicken.
2. When oil is hot, add onions and sauté until soft.
3. Add garlic, chili powder, and sea salt.
4. Pour in salsa and add rice, broth, and black beans.
5. Close lid and lock. Set to "rice" and adjust for 10 minutes.
6. When done, quick release until all pressure is released.
7. Open and stir mixture. Top with cilantro and cheddar cheese. Serve.

Meats

CHICKEN FAJITAS

Serves 4

Ingredients:

- 1T extra-virgin olive oil
- 1lb chicken breasts, boneless, skinless
- 2 large onions, diced
- 8 cloves garlic, minced
- 1 red bell pepper, cut into strips
- 1 green bell pepper, cut into strips
- 1 (15-oz) can diced tomatoes, drained
- 1 jalapeño, chopped (optional)
- ¼t pepper flakes
- 8 corn tortillas, warmed

Instructions:

1. Set to "sear" and add oil.
2. When oil is hot, add chicken, onions, and garlic and sauté until meat is lightly browned.
3. Stir in tomatoes, bell pepper, and chili peppers.
4. Close lid and lock. Set to "poultry" and adjust for 5 minutes.
5. When done, quick release until all pressure is released.
6. Open and spoon chicken and pepper mixture onto warmed tortillas and serve.
7. Top with jalapeños (optional).

Meats

BRAISED LAMB SHANKS
WITH ROOT VEGETABLES

Serves 6

Ingredients:

- 4-6 lamb shanks, French trimmed, excess fat removed, if possible
- 2 tomatoes, peeled, each cut into eighths
- 4t plain flour (optional, for thickening gravy)
- ¼c plain flour
- 2t olive oil
- 1 onion, diced
- 3 carrots, peeled, thinly sliced
- 1 garlic clove, crushed
- 1T fresh oregano, chopped (or 1t dried oregano)
- 1t lemon rind, finely grated
- ¾c red wine
- 2c beef stock (or vegetable stock)
-   Sea salt
-   Freshly ground black pepper

Instructions:

1. Toss shanks in flour, shake off excess.
2. Set to "sear" and heat the oil in pressure cooker (without lid). Place lamb shanks in and brown on both sides.
3. Remove shanks; set aside.
4. Add onions, carrots, and garlic, and sauté for 5 minutes, stirring occasionally.
5. Add tomatoes, oregano, lemon, wine, and stock. Bring to boil, stirring well, for a few minutes.
6. Return the lamb to the cooker and season well with sea salt and fresh ground pepper.
7. Close lid and lock. Set to "meat/stew" and adjust for 25 minutes.
8. When done, quick release until all pressure is released.
9. Carefully open and check to see if meat is cooked. The lamb should be very tender and be almost falling off the bone.
10. Simmer to reduce broth until it thickens.
11. Serve lamb with mashed potatoes and vegetables.

Meats

CHICKEN ADOBO

Serves 5

Ingredients:

8-10 chicken legs and thighs
2T   oil
1   onion, sliced
5-10 cloves garlic, chopped
4   bay leaves
      Freshly ground black pepper
1T   brown sugar
½c   soy sauce
¼c   rice vinegar
¼c   apple cider vinegar

For yellow rice:

1c   yellow rice
1½c water

Instructions:

1. Set to "sear" and add oil.
2. When oil is hot, place chicken in and sear on both sides. Remove to plate; set aside.
3. Add onions and sauté until soft.
4. Add garlic and remaining ingredients. Bring up to a simmer.
5. Return chicken to cooker.
6. Close lid and lock. Set to "poultry" and adjust for 12 minutes.
7. When done, natural release. Allow sauce to thicken. Afterward, quick release until all pressure is released.
8. Open and serve chicken on top of cooked yellow rice.

Tip: For the yellow rice, cook before making chicken and adobo sauce, cover, and then set aside. To make, add uncooked yellow rice and 1c water to pressure cooker, close lid and lock, and set to "rice" for 8 minutes. When done, natural release for 35 minutes. Afterward, quick release until all pressure is released, open, and then fluff rice with a fork.

Meats

BRAISED TURKEY THIGHS
WITH YUKON GOLD POTATOES & CRANBERRIES

Serves 4

Ingredients:

- 3T olive oil
- 4 turkey thighs, skinless
- 1 large carrot, peeled, diced
- 1 large celery, diced
- 1 medium onion, diced
- 4 large cloves garlic, minced
- 1lb Yukon Gold potatoes, cleaned, chopped
- 1c fresh cranberries
- 1T tomato paste
- 1c dry white wine
- 1c water
- 1 (14 ½-oz) can whole tomatoes, crushed, in juice
- 2t dried thyme
- 1T dried marjoram leaves
- 1T dried rosemary leaves
- 1 bay leaf
- Sea salt
- Freshly ground black pepper

Instructions:

1. Set to "sear" and add oil.
2. Season turkey thighs with sea salt and fresh ground black pepper.
3. Place turkey thighs in and sear on both sides until golden brown. Remove and put on a plate; set aside.
4. Add onions, carrot, celery, and cranberries to oil and sauté for a couple minutes.
5. Add garlic and tomato paste and stir well. Add wine and water to deglaze the bottom of cooker.
6. Add tomatoes, thyme, marjoram, rosemary, bay leaf, sea salt, and fresh ground black pepper. Stir well.
7. Return chicken thighs to cooker.
8. Close lid and lock. Set to "poultry" and adjust for 7 minutes.
9. When done, quick release until all pressure is released.
10. Open and set to "potato". Add potatoes and cook for an additional 10 minutes. When done, remove bay leaf and serve.

Meats

BEEF OSSO BUCO
WITH GREMOLATA

Serves 6

Ingredients:

- 6   thick beef shank slices (1½ to 2 inches thick, about 3lbs)
- 1t   vegetable oil
- 3t   kosher salt
- 1½t   freshly ground black pepper
- 1   large onion, diced
- 1   stalk celery, diced
- 1   carrot, diced
- 4   garlic cloves, crushed
- 1T   tomato paste
- 2   sprigs thyme (or 1t dried thyme)
- ½t   kosher salt
- 1c   chicken stock (preferably homemade)
- ½c   dry white wine
- 1   (15-oz) can diced tomatoes

Gremolata:

- 1   garlic clove, minced
-     Zest of 2 lemons
- 1c   parsley (leaves only)

Instructions:

1. Trim fat off outsides of beef shanks and season with 3t of kosher salt and fresh ground black pepper.
2. Set to "sear" and add vegetable oil.
3. Place half the shanks in and sear for 3 minutes per side until well browned.
4. Remove shanks and place in a bowl. Add the second half of shanks and repeat, including removing to bowl.
5. Remove (pour or ladle out) all but 1T of the oil and fat in the cooker.
6. Add onions, celery, carrot, garlic, tomato paste, and thyme to cooker.
7. Sprinkle with ½t of kosher salt and sauté until onions are soft, about 5 minutes.
8. Add chicken stock and wine to deglaze bottom of cooker, loosening any browned bits.
9. Return beef and any liquid back to pressure cooker and pour tomatoes on top.
10. Close lid and lock. Set to "meat/stew" and adjust for 30 minutes.
11. In a small bowl, add minced garlic, lemon zest, and parsley leaves to make gremolata. Combine well.
12. When beef shanks are done, natural release for 15 minutes.
13. Afterward, quick release until all pressure is released.
14. Open and remove beef from cooker and transfer to plate. Cover with foil and let rest.
15. Pour (or ladle out) liquid sauce from pressure cooker into a glass fat separator. Let liquid rest for about 10 minutes to allow for fat to surface.
16. When fat rises, pour remaining separated liquid into a gravy boat.
17. To serve, plate one shank, pour some sauce over the top, and sprinkle gremolata on top.

Meats

CHICKEN POT PIE

Serves 4

Ingredients:

- 2 lbs chicken breasts, boneless, skinless
- ¼ c onions, diced fine
- 1 lb mixed vegetables
- 1 (8-oz) can biscuit dough, quartered
- 3 potatoes, peeled, cut into chunks
- 1 c celery root, large dice
- ¼ t freshly ground black pepper
- 1 qt chicken stock
- 1 can cream of chicken soup
- 2 t seasoned salt

Instructions:

1. In a bowl, mix cream of chicken soup, seasoned salt, and fresh ground pepper; set aside.
2. Set to "sear" and place chicken breasts in pressure cooker. Add chicken stock and onions.
3. Add potatoes, celery root, and vegetables. Pour in cream of chicken soup mix.
4. Place quartered biscuit dough on top. Sprinkle seasoned salt over biscuits.
5. Close lid and lock. Set to "time" and adjust for 4 minutes.
6. When done, natural release for 35 minutes. Afterward, quick release until all pressure is released.
7. Open and serve.

Meats

CHICKEN PUTTANESCA

Serves 6

Ingredients:

- 6 chicken thighs, skin on
- 2T olive oil
- 2 cloves garlic, crushed
- ½t chili flakes
- 1 (14½-oz) can chopped tomatoes
- 6oz pitted black olives
- 1T capers, rinsed, drained
- 1T basil, chopped
- ¾c water

Instructions:

1. Set to "sear" and add oil.
2. Place chicken thighs in skin side down and cook for 5 minutes. When done, remove chicken; set aside.
3. Add in tomatoes, water, olives, garlic, capers, basil, and chili flakes. Bring up to a simmer.
4. Return chicken to cooker.
5. Close lid and lock. Set to "poultry" and adjust for 15 minutes.
6. When done, natural release for 35 minutes. Afterward, quick release until all pressure is released.
7. Open and remove chicken. Serve.

Meats

CHORIZO & CHICKEN
WITH CUBAN RICE

Serves 4

Ingredients:

10	chicken thighs, bone-in, skin on	½lb	fully cooked Spanish chorizo, cut into ¼-inch-thick rounds
¼c	fresh lime juice	2c	finely chopped onions
¼c	cilantro, with stems, minced	½c	chopped red bell pepper
2T	olive oil	3	garlic cloves, chopped
1T	finely grated lime peel	2c	Arborio rice
1T	chopped fresh thyme	2½c	low-sodium chicken broth, plus ½c (if needed, to add moisture to rice)
2t	chopped, seeded jalapeño chili	2	medium tomatoes, diced
2t	Hungarian sweet paprika	¼t	saffron threads
2t	freshly ground black pepper	1	canned piquillo pepper, cut into thin strips
1t	ground cumin	½c	cilantro, coarsely chopped
½t	sea salt		
¼t	ground allspice		
1T	olive oil		

Instructions:

1. In a medium bowl, whisk lime juice, cilantro, 2T olive oil, lime peel, thyme, jalapeño, paprika, fresh ground pepper, cumin, sea salt, and allspice for the marinade.
2. Place chicken and marinade in a large resealable plastic bag. Turn several times to coat chicken. Refrigerate at least 4 hours up to 24 hours.
3. When ready to cook, heat 1T of the olive oil in heavy, large, wide pot over medium heat.
4. Add chorizo and sauté until brown and fat begins to render, about 3 minutes.
5. Using slotted spoon, transfer chorizo to a medium bowl.
6. In the pressure cooker, set to "sear" and add half of the chicken, skin-side down. Cook until brown, about 5 minutes per side.
7. Remove chicken and transfer to plate; set aside.
8. Repeat with remaining chicken thighs.
9. Pour off all but 3T of fat from the pressure cooker, discarding the excess fat. Add onions and sauté for 4 minutes, scraping up any browned bits.
10. Add bell pepper and garlic and sauté until onions are translucent, about 2 minutes.
11. Mix in Arborio rice, stirring to blend with vegetables.
12. Add broth, tomatoes (with any juice), saffron, and reserved marinade. Bring up to a boil. Stir well.
13. Return chicken, add chorizo, and any accumulated juices to cooker, pressing chicken partially into rice.
14. Set to "sear" and adjust for 15 minutes.
15. Arrange piquillo pepper strips over chicken, cover, and continue to simmer for 10 minutes until chicken is cooked and rice is tender. Add additional broth to keep rice moist, if needed.
16. Serve in large shallow bowl with cilantro and lime wedges.

Meats

CHICKEN TIKKA MASALA

Serves 6

Ingredients:

1½ lbs chicken thighs, boneless, skinless
1½ T olive oil
1 onion, diced
3 cloves garlic, minced
1 piece ginger, grated
½ c chicken broth
1½ T garam masala
1 t smoked paprika
½ t ground turmeric
½ t sea salt
¼ t cayenne pepper
1 can diced tomatoes
½ c heavy cream (or coconut milk, optional)
2 c cooked basmati rice

Instructions:

1. Set to "sear" and add oil.
2. When oil is hot, add onions, garlic, ginger and sauté.
3. Add ¼ c of the chicken broth. Cook down and reduce liquid by half.
4. Add garam masala, paprika, turmeric, sea salt, and cayenne pepper.
5. Add chicken thighs, tomatoes, and the remaining ¼ c chicken broth.
6. Close lid and lock. Set to "poultry" and adjust for 13 minutes.
7. When done, quick release until all pressure is released.
8. Open and add heavy cream or coconut milk (optional) to sauce. Top with cilantro and serve over cooked basmati rice.

Meats

CHICKEN TINGA
FROM MEXICO

Serves 6

Ingredients:

- 1T vegetable oil
- ½ large sweet onion, diced
- 2 garlic cloves, minced
- 1 large tomatillo, diced
- 1t ground cumin
- 1t dried Mexican oregano
- 1t sea salt
- 1 (15-oz) can fire-roasted, diced tomatoes, with liquid
- ¼c water
- 2 chipotle chilies in adobo sauce, minced
- 1T cayenne pepper sauce
- 3 large uncooked chicken breasts, diced
- 1 (15-oz) can black or pinto beans, drained, rinsed
- 6 12-inch flour tortillas, warmed
- 4oz cheddar cheese, grated

Instructions:

1. Set to "sear" and add oil.
2. When oil is hot, add onions and sauté until soft, about 3 minutes.
3. Add tomatillo, cumin, oregano, garlic, and sea salt, stirring constantly for an additional 3 minutes.
4. Add tomatoes, water, chipotle chilies, and cayenne pepper sauce.
5. Using a stick (immersion) blender, puree soup until very smooth.
6. Stir in chicken.
7. Close lid and lock. Set to "time" and adjust for 4 minutes.
8. When done, quick release until all pressure is released.
9. Open. Set to "sear" and cook, stirring occasionally and gently until sauce clings to chicken and most of liquid has evaporated.
10. While cooking, mash beans with fork until chunky.
11. Serve by spooning chicken mixture onto tortillas, adding beans, and sprinkling cheddar cheese on top.

Meats

CHICKEN CACCIATORE
(HUNTER STYLE)

Serves 6

Ingredients:

- 2T   extra-virgin olive oil
- 2lbs chicken thighs, boneless, with skin on
- 1   large onion, minced
- 3   garlic cloves, minced
- 1t   dried oregano
- ¼t   red pepper flakes
- 1   bay leaf
- 1   (28-oz) can diced tomatoes
- ¼c low-sodium chicken broth (or white wine)
- 2   green bell peppers, cut into 1-inch squares
-      Sea salt
-      Freshly ground black pepper
- ½lbs sliced mushrooms

Instructions:

1. Set to "sear" and adjust for 12 minutes and add olive oil.
2. Season chicken thighs with sea salt and fresh ground pepper.
3. Working in batches, sear chicken on all sides until golden brown, adding more oil if necessary. Remove chicken and set aside.
4. Add onions, mushrooms, and sauté until tender, scraping up browned bits, about 4 minutes.
5. Add garlic, oregano, and red pepper flakes and cook about 1 minute.
6. Add bay leaf, tomatoes, and chicken broth. Return chicken to cooker. Press chicken into and under tomatoes until submerged.
7. Close lid and lock. Set to "poultry" and adjust for 10 minutes.
8. When done, quick release until all pressure is released.
9. Open and add green peppers. Stir.
10. Close lid and lock. Set to "steam/veggies" and adjust for 2 minutes.
11. When done, quick release until all pressure is released.
12. Open and discard bay leaf. Season to taste with sea salt and fresh ground black pepper.

Tip: Serve over rice or pasta.

Meats

CHICKEN
WITH COCONUT CURRY

Serves 4

Ingredients:

- 2 lbs chicken breast, boneless, skinless, cut into 1-inch cubes
- 1 T sugar
- 1 (8-oz) can tomato sauce
- 1 (14-oz) can light coconut milk
- ½ t freshly ground black pepper
- 1 t sea salt
- 2 c Roma tomatoes, chopped
- 1 T garlic, minced
- ½ c onions, sliced thin
- 2 T curry powder
- 1 T olive oil or ghee
- 1 t ginger

Instructions:

1. Set to "sear" and add oil.
2. When oil is hot, add chicken and brown the meat. Add curry powder and stir constantly.
3. Add onions, garlic, and ginger. Cook an additional 30 seconds.
4. Add tomatoes, sea salt, fresh ground black pepper, coconut milk, tomato sauce, and sugar.
5. Close lid and lock. Set to "meat/stew" and adjust for 10 minutes.
6. When done, quick release until all pressure is released.
7. Open and season with sea salt and fresh ground pepper.
8. Close lid and lock. Set for 5 minutes.
9. When done, quick release until all pressure is released.
10. Serve chicken curry with basmati rice or quinoa.

Meats

CHICKEN
WITH ITALIAN SEASONING

Serves 6

Ingredients:

4lbs chicken breasts
1T   Italian seasoning
½t   sea salt
½t   freshly ground black pepper
1c   chicken broth

Instructions:

1. Place chicken in pressure cooker and brown chicken on both sides. Season with Italian seasoning, sea salt, and fresh ground pepper. Pour chicken broth over top.
2. Close lid and lock. Set to "poultry" and adjust for 18 minutes.
3. When done, natural release for 35 minutes. Afterward, quick release until all pressure is released.
4. Open. Remove chicken and place on platter.

Meats

CHICKEN MOLE

Serves 4

Ingredients:

1L	(4¼c) water	½t	ground cloves
3	ancho chilies, dried, seeds removed	4-5	cloves of garlic
3	pasilla chilies, dried, seeds removed	6	cinnamon sticks
3	mulato chilies dried, seeds removed	2T	tomato paste
3	guajillo chilies, dried, seeds removed	½c	chocolate
3	chipotle chilies, dried, seeds removed	1	medium-sweet onion, diced
3	morita chilies, dried, seeds removed	1c	vegetable oil
2T	sesame seeds		Sea salt
1t	ground cumin		Freshly ground black pepper
1T	fresh oregano	2c	chicken broth
1t	caraway seeds		
1T	fresh thyme		
1t	ground nutmeg		

Instructions:

1. Set to "sear" and add oil.
2. When oil is hot, add onions and garlic. Sauté until golden brown.
3. Add chilies and stir constantly to coat with the oil.
4. Add water, all spices, and herbs.
5. Add chicken broth, cinnamon, seeds, chocolate, and tomato paste to cooker.
6. Close lid and lock. Set to "soup" and adjust for 20 minutes.
7. When done, quick release until all pressure is released.
8. Working in small batches, ladle each into a blender. Puree each batch.
9. Return blended, pureed sauce to cooker.
10. Set to "sear" and add remaining oil. Blend with oil and stir constantly. Do not let sauce burn. If consistency is too thick, add 1 or 2c of the chicken broth.

Tip: Boil chicken separately and serve the sauce on top or make tacos and top as you would with salsa.

Meats

CORNED BEEF & CABBAGE

Serves 6

Ingredients:

4c water
2½-lb point-cut corned beef brisket
3   garlic cloves, quartered
2   bay leaves
4   carrots, cut into 3-inch pieces
1   head cabbage, cut into 6 wedges
6   potatoes, peeled, quartered
3   turnips, peeled, quartered
     Horseradish sauce (optional)

Instructions:

1. Set to "sear" and pour water into pressure cooker. Add brisket.
2. Bring water up to a rolling boil.
3. Skim residue from surface.
4. Add garlic and bay leaves.
5. Close lid and lock. Set to "meat/stew" and adjust for 1 hour, 15 minutes.
6. When done, quick release until all pressure is released.
7. Open and add vegetables to brisket and cooking liquid, stirring gently.
8. Close lid and lock. Set to "potatoes" for 6 minutes.
9. When done, quick release until all pressure is released.
10. Open. Remove corned beef and transfer to a platter or cutting board. Cover loosely with foil. Let rest for 5 minutes.
11. Slice across the grain. Serve with horseradish sauce (optional).

Meats

EASTER HAM

Serves 6

Ingredients:

10-lb ham
½c brown sugar
30 whole cloves
1c pineapple juice
1c brown mustard

Instructions:

1. In a bowl, mix pineapple juice, brown sugar, and brown mustard; set aside.
2. Score (carve lines down) the ham with a knife. Insert cloves inside each cut.
3. Place ham inside the cooker. Pour half the mixture from the bowl onto the ham; reserve the other half.
4. Close lid and lock. Set to "meat/stew" and adjust for 1 hour.
5. When done, quick release until all pressure is released.
6. Open and remove ham. Use the reserved glaze from the bowl and brush onto ham. Brush any cooked glaze from the cooker onto ham as well.

Meats

CIDER-BRAISED PORK STEW

Serves 6

Ingredients:

- 3-lb pork shoulder, cut into 1-inch cubes
- 1t kosher salt
- 1T vegetable oil
- 1 large onion, diced
- 1 Granny Smith apple (optional), peeled, diced
- ½t kosher salt
- 12oz hard cider (or substitute non-alcoholic cider)
- 1 sprig fresh sage (or ½t dried sage)
- 1 sprig fresh thyme (or ½t dried thyme)
- 1lb carrots, peeled, cut lengthwise into 3-inch strips (or use baby carrots)
- 1½lbs new potatoes, scrubbed
- Sea salt
- Freshly ground black pepper
- Parsley, minced (for garnish)

Instructions:

1. Set to "sear" and add oil. Heat until oil is shimmering.
2. Season pork with 1t of the kosher salt. Add pork to pressure cooker and brown the meat.
3. Remove pork, leaving as much fat as possible in the bottom of cooker.
4. Add onions and apples. Stir to coat. Add ½t of the kosher salt. Sauté, scraping browned bits of pork from bottom of pan, about 8 minutes or until onions are tender.
5. Pour cider into pot and bring up to a boil for 1 minute.
6. Return pork and any juices from bowl to pressure cooker and stir. Coat pork with cider and onions.
7. Add sage and thyme sprigs.
8. Rest a steamer basket on top of contents in cooker. Add potatoes and carrots to the steamer basket.
9. Close lid and lock. Set "meat/stew" and adjust for 24 minutes.
10. When done, natural release for 20 minutes. Afterward, quick release until all pressure is released.
11. Open and lift steamer basket out of cooker. Discard sage and thyme sprigs.
12. Allow potatoes to cool for 1 minute, then remove from basket and cut each in half.
13. Return carrots from basket and halved potatoes to cooker and into stew. Add sea salt and fresh ground black pepper to taste. Sprinkle with chopped parsley and serve.

Meats

INDIAN BUTTER CHICKEN

Serves 4

Ingredients:

- 2 lbs chicken breast, diced
- ½ c butter
- 2 t garam masala
- 2 t curry powder
- 1 t ground cumin
- 1 t ground ginger
- 1 can coconut milk
- 1 c chicken stock
- 1 (60-oz) can tomato paste
- 1 onion, minced
- Sea salt
- 2 T cornstarch
- 1 T water

Instructions:

1. Set to "sear" and add butter.
2. When butter has melted, add onion, cooking only partially.
3. Add curry, cumin, ginger, garam masala, and sea salt.
4. Place chicken in pot. Mix coconut milk, stock, and tomato paste. Pour over chicken.
5. Close and lock lid. Set to "poultry" and adjust for 15 minutes.
6. When done, quick release until all pressure is released.
7. In a bowl, mix cornstarch and water.
8. Open cooker and add mixture to thicken the sauce. Serve.

Meats

ITALIAN BEEF

Serves 4

Ingredients:

3 lbs beef chuck, cubed
2t dried oregano
1t dried basil
1t onion powder
1t paprika
1t freshly ground black pepper
½t rosemary
½t thyme
½t red pepper flakes
½t garlic powder
1T oil
1 onion, thinly sliced
3 cloves garlic, minced
2c beef stock

Instructions:

1. In a bowl, add oregano, basil, onion powder, paprika, fresh ground pepper, rosemary, thyme, red pepper, and garlic powder. Mix well.
2. Place beef in another bowl and sprinkle with the mixed spices. Blend well to coat the beef.
3. In the cooker, set to "sear" and add oil.
4. When oil is hot, add onions and garlic and sauté for 1 minute.
5. Add in the beef and stir. Add beef stock.
6. Close lid and lock. Set to "meat/stew" and adjust for 30 minutes.
7. When done, natural release for 35 minutes. Afterward, quick release until all pressure is released.
8. Open and carefully transfer beef to a bowl. Shred or slice the meat.
9. Return beef to cooker and allow to soak in cooking juice.

Tip: Make sandwiches with the Italian beef and add favorite toppings.

Meats

CUBAN ROPA VIEJA

Serves 4

Ingredients:

- 2 lbs sirloin tip roast, cut into 6 large chunks
- 1½t sea salt
- ¾t freshly ground black pepper
- ¼c avocado oil (or ghee)
- 1 large yellow onion, halved, thinly sliced
- 2 red, orange, and/or yellow bell peppers, stemmed, seeds removed, and sliced into thin strips
- 5 garlic cloves, minced
- 2t dried oregano
- 2t cumin
- 1½t smoked paprika
- ½t turmeric
- ¼c dry white wine
- 2 (4-oz) boxes, organic tomatoes, strained
- 2 bay leaves
- ¼c capers, rinsed, drained
- ¼c chopped, jarred pimiento peppers, rinsed, drained
- ½c golden raisins
- 1T sherry vinegar (or white wine vinegar)

Instructions:

1. Season beef on all sides with sea salt and fresh ground black pepper.
2. Set to "sear" and heat avocado oil.
3. When oil is hot, add beef and brown for 10 minutes, turning pieces halfway. Transfer beef to plate.
4. Add onions and peppers in pressure cooker and sauté, stirring frequently for 3-4 minutes until somewhat softened.
5. Stir in garlic, oregano, and spices, and cook for 1 minute.
6. Pour in wine and let it reduce for 2-3 minutes until most of liquid is gone.
7. Add tomatoes and bay leaves. Return beef with juices to pressure cooker and stir.
8. Close lid and lock. Set to "meat/stew" for 40 minutes.
9. When done, quick release until all pressure is released.
10. Open. Remove beef to plate. Using 2 forks, shred the beef.
11. Remove bay leaves and return the beef to pressure cooker.
12. Add capers, pimientos, raisins, and sherry vinegar, and stir.
13. Set to "sear" and adjust for 10 minutes. Cook until sauce is thickened.

Tip: Serve with rice, guacamole, or fried plantains.

JAMAICAN-STYLE OXTAIL

Serves 2

Ingredients:

- 1lb beef oxtail, cut into pieces
- 1 large onion, chopped
- 1 green onion, thinly sliced
- 2 garlic cloves, minced
- 1t minced fresh ginger root
- 2T soy sauce
- 1 sprig fresh thyme, chopped
- ½t sea salt
- 1t freshly ground black pepper
- 2T vegetable oil
- 1½c water
- 1c canned fava beans, drained
- 1t whole allspice berries
- 1T cornstarch
- 2T water

Instructions:

1. Set to "sear" and add onions, green onions, garlic, ginger, soy sauce, thyme, sea salt, and fresh ground pepper.
2. Heat vegetable oil in a large skillet over medium-high heat.
3. Place oxtail in skillet and brown all over, about 10 minutes.
4. Place oxtail into pressure cooker and pour in 1½c of water.
5. Close lid and lock. Set to "meat/stew" and adjust for 25 minutes.
6. When done, quick release until all pressure is released. Open and add fava beans and allspice berries. Bring up to a simmer.
7. In a small bowl, dissolve cornstarch in the 2T of the water and add to cooker.
8. Stir. Close lid and lock. Set cooker to "meat/stew" and adjust for 35 minutes.
9. When done, quick release until all pressure is released. Open. Cook and stir a few minutes longer until sauce has thickened and beans are tender.

Meats

GREEN CHILI PORK STEW

Serves 4

Ingredients:

- 3 lbs pork shoulder, fat trimmed, meat cut into 2-inch cubes
- 4T canola oil
- Sea salt and freshly ground pepper
- 1t cumin
- ¼t cayenne pepper
- 4 cloves of garlic, finely minced
- 1 red onion, finely diced
- 1½ lbs fresh tomatillos
- 1 fresh jalapeño, seeds removed
- 2c chicken broth

Instructions:

1. Set to "sear" and add 2T of the oil.
2. Season pork with sea salt and fresh ground pepper. Place pork in and brown the meat.
3. Add chicken broth.
4. Close lid and lock. Set to "meat/stew" and adjust for 15 minutes.
5. When done, quick release until all pressure is released.
6. Open and remove pork and liquid; set aside.
7. Clean the pot.
8. Set to "sear" and add remaining 2T of oil. Add onions and sauté until light brown.
9. Add garlic and jalapeño and cook until fragrant.
10. Add tomatillos, cayenne pepper, and cumin. Return pork meat with the liquid to stew.
11. Close lid and lock. Set to "time" and adjust for 7 minutes.
12. When done, quick release until all pressure is released.
13. Open, stir, and serve.

Meats

GREEN CHILI PULLED PORK CARNITAS

Serves 8

Ingredients:

- 1 (5-lb) pork shoulder or pork butt, skin removed, cut into pieces
- 4 large oranges
- 1 lime
- 1 large onion, chopped
- 10 garlic cloves, minced
- 1 large jalapeño pepper, stems and seeds removed, with pepper chopped
- 2 cinnamon sticks
- 2 bay leaves
- 1-2T extra-virgin olive oil
-   Juice from pork, fat skimmed

Pork Rub:
- 2T kosher salt
- 1T ground cumin
- 2t dried oregano
- ¼t freshly ground black pepper

Garnish:
- Limes
- Pico de gallo
- Fresh cilantro
- Avocado

Instructions:

1. Remove skin and bone from pork shoulder, and cut into 8-10 pieces. Place in a bowl. Add rub ingredients, and massage into pork.
2. Set to "sear" and sauté 3 lbs of the pork fat for 3 minutes.
3. Add the juice of 1 orange and deglaze bottom of cooker. Turn off heat.
4. Place pork in pot and add onions, garlic, jalapeño, cinnamon sticks, and bay leaves.
5. Add the juice of 1 orange and deglaze bottom of cooker. Turn off heat.
6. Close lid and lock. Set to "meat/stew" and adjust for 40 minutes.
7. When done, natural release for 20 minutes. Afterward, quick release until all pressure is released.
8. Open. Remove meat from cooker and strain liquid.
9. Shred pork well.
10. Return meat to pressure cooker and set to "sear." Sauté meat for 10 minutes, reducing the liquid.
11. Pour liquid into a large measuring cup and skim off the fat.
12. Heat a pan on medium-high heat.
13. Add olive oil and some of the shredded pork to the pan.
14. Cook for 1 minute then add ½c of the hot (carnitas) liquid. Fry on one side until liquid has evaporated. Repeat until all pork is done.
15. To serve, place carnitas on platter, drizzle with the carnitas liquid, fresh lime juice, and sprinkle with chopped cilantro. Remove bay leaves before serving.

Meats

KALUA PIG

Serves 6

Ingredients:

- 3 slices of bacon
- 5-lb bone-in pork shoulder roast
- 3 garlic cloves, peeled
- 1½T sea salt
- 1c water
- 1 head of cabbage, cut into wedges
- Salt
- 2T liquid smoke

Instructions:

1. Set to "sear" and add bacon and sauté.
2. Slice pork roast into 3 pieces, cut a slit in each piece, and then stuff each with garlic cloves and salt.
3. Place pork on top of bacon. Add water and liquid smoke.
4. Close lid and lock. Set to "meat/stew" and adjust for 90 minutes.
5. When done, natural release for 35 minutes. Afterward, quick release until all pressure is released.
6. Open. Remove pork and place in a bowl or on platter. Cover; set aside.
7. Add cabbage to cooker. Close lid and lock. Set for 4 minutes.
8. When done, quick release until all pressure is released.
9. Shred the pork with a fork.
10. Open cooker and add pork with cabbage. Serve.

Meats

LEMON-BUTTER CHICKEN
WITH FRESH HERBS

Serves 6

Ingredients:

- 6 chicken breasts, skin on
- 4 cloves of garlic, peeled
- 3T olive oil
- ½c chicken stock
- 2-3 lemons (juice only)
- 4 carrots
- 1t oregano
- 1t parsley flakes
- 1 onion, sliced
- Sea salt
- Freshly ground black pepper
- ½ stick of butter

Instructions:

1. Set to "sear" and add oil.
2. Season chicken breasts with sea salt and fresh ground black pepper. Place chicken breasts in cooker, skin side down, and sear until golden brown, about 5 minutes. Flip and cook other side for 5 minutes.
3. Add garlic, onions, carrots, and butter. Sauté for 2-3 minutes, add the stock, oregano, and lemon juice.
4. Close lid and lock. Set to "poultry" and adjust for 10 minutes.
5. When done, quick release until all pressure is released.

Tip: You have the option of serving chicken "as is" or you can place cooked breasts on a roasting pan and broil in regular oven for 5 minutes, or less (watching, checking constantly), to get the skin crispy.

Meats

KOREAN SHORT RIBS

Serves 6

Ingredients:

- 1t vegetable oil
- 2 green onions, cut into 1-inch lengths
- 3 garlic cloves, smashed
- 3 quarter-sized slices of ginger
- 4 lbs beef short ribs, about 3 inches thick, cut into 3 rib portions
- ½c water
- ½c soy sauce
- ¼c rice wine (or dry sherry)
- ¼c pear juice (or apple juice)
- 2t sesame oil

Garnish:

- 2 green onions, minced
-    Gochujang sauce (optional)
-    Sesame seeds (optional)

Instructions:

1. Set to "sear" and add vegetable oil in the pressure cooker and heat until the oil is shimmering.
2. Add the green onion, garlic, and ginger, and sauté for 1 minute.
3. Add short ribs, water, soy sauce, rice wine, pear juice, and sesame oil, stirring until ribs are completely coated.
4. Close lid and lock. Set to "meat/stew" and adjust for 45 minutes.
5. When done, natural release for at least 15 minutes.
6. When done, quick release until all pressure is released.
7. Open and remove ribs from pot with a slotted spoon.
8. Pour remaining liquid into a fat separator and let it settle, allowing the fat to float to the surface.
9. Serve ribs with the degreased sauce.
10. Garnish ribs with additional minced green onions, Gochujang sauce, and sesame seeds (optional).

Tip: If time allows, boil degreased sauce over high heat until reduced by half to thicken.

Meats

MY MOM'S MEATLOAF

Serves 8

Ingredients:

- 2 lbs lean ground beef
- ½c Italian breadcrumbs
- ¼c grated Parmesan cheese
- ¼c finely minced yellow onion
- 1 large egg, beaten
- 1T minced garlic
- 2t Worcestershire sauce
- ½t dried thyme
- 1t sea salt
- ½t freshly ground black pepper
- 1T vegetable oil
- 1 yellow onion, diced
- 1c ketchup (or BBQ sauce)
- ½c beef stock (or broth)

Instructions:

1. In a large bowl, combine beef, breadcrumbs, cheese, minced yellow onion, beaten egg, garlic, Worcestershire sauce, thyme, sea salt, and fresh ground pepper.
2. Form mixture into a round loaf that will fit into pressure cooker; set aside.
3. Set to "sear" and add oil.
4. Add yellow onions to cooker and sauté until translucent, or 4-5 minutes.
5. Stir in ketchup and beef stock. Top with rounded meatloaf.
6. Close lid and lock. Set to "meat/stew" and adjust for 15 minutes.
7. When done, natural release, 10 minutes.
8. Afterward, quick release until all pressure is released.
9. Open and remove meatloaf, slice, and serve.

Meats

NAVARIN OF LAMB

Serves 6

Ingredients:

6-8	lamb shoulder
	Sea Salt and freshly ground black pepper
¼c	plain flour
1T	butter
2T	tomato paste
½c	white wine (optional, or use extra stock)
2 c	chicken stock
3	fresh thyme sprigs (or 1t dried thyme)
1	sprig rosemary
3	bay leaves
4	garlic cloves, chopped
1	(16-oz) can chopped tomatoes
½lb	baby carrots, peeled, chopped
2	spring onions, cut into thirds
1½c	green beans, trimmed
1c	peas
⅔lb	(9-12) new potatoes, each halved

Instructions:

1. Season lamb with sea salt and fresh ground black pepper.
2. Place flour in bag with lamb and toss to coat.
3. Heat butter over high heat in a large saucepan.
4. Sear lamb a few at a time. Brown on both sides; set aside.
5. Add tomato paste to the saucepan, cook for a few minutes on high heat. (Optional: if using wine, add, and let sauce bubble for 30 seconds.)
6. Place lamb in pressure cooker and add stock, thyme, rosemary sprig, bay leaves, garlic, remaining veggies, and sauce from the saucepan.
7. Close lid and lock. Set to "meat/stew" and adjust for 15 minutes.
8. When done, quick release until all pressure is released.
9. Open. Vegetables should be tender and lamb, fork tender. Add a little oil, and add sea salt and fresh ground black pepper to taste. Serve lamb with the vegetables from the stew on top.

Meats

KUNG PAO CHICKEN

Serves 4

Ingredients:

1 lb	chicken breast, cut into bite-sized cubes
2 c	white rice, cooked according to package directions

Kung Pao Sauce:
- 3T peanut oil (or vegetable oil)
- 2T white sesame seeds
- 2t Korean chili flakes
- 1t ground Sichuan peppercorns
- 8 garlic cloves, minced
- 2 large slices ginger, minced
- ½c Chinkiang vinegar
- ¼c light soy sauce (or soy sauce)
- ¼c Shaoxing wine (or dry sherry or water)
- ⅓c sugar
- 1T cornstarch
- ½t coarse sea salt (or ¼t fine sea salt)
- Sesame seeds
- Freshly ground black pepper
- 1 green onion, thin slice (for garnish)

Instructions:

1. For the sauce, in a bowl, combine Chinkiang vinegar, light soy sauce, Shaoxing wine, sugar, cornstarch, and sea salt. Stir to dissolve; set aside.
2. In a saucepan, add peanut oil, chili pepper flakes, and sesame seeds. Cook over medium-low heat until sizzling. Cook and stir until seeds turn dark brown and release their oil.
3. Add ground Sichuan peppercorns, garlic, and ginger to saucepan. Cook and stir for an additional 30 seconds.
4. Add sauce from the bowl and pour into the saucepan. Cook and stir until sauce thickens just enough to coat a wooden spoon. Add sea salt and fresh ground pepper to taste. Pour all sauce back into the bowl.
5. Place chicken cubes into pressure cooker. Pour sauce from bowl over the top of chicken.
6. Close lid and lock. Set to "poultry" and adjust for 15 minutes.
7. While chicken is cooking, prepare rice.
8. When chicken is done, quick release until all pressure is released.
9. Open. Serve over cooked rice. Garnish with green onions.

Meats

ORANGE CHICKEN

Serves 4

Ingredients:

- 4 chicken breasts, boneless, skinless, diced
- ¼c soy sauce
- ¼c water
- 2T brown sugar
- 1T rice wine vinegar
- 1t sesame oil
- ¼t chili sauce
- ½c orange marmalade
- 3T cornstarch
- 2 green onions, chopped

Instructions:

1. Set to "sear" and add sesame oil.
2. When oil is hot, add chicken, soy sauce, brown sugar, vinegar, and chili sauce. Stir.
3. Close lid and lock. Set to "poultry" and adjust for 5 minutes.
4. When done, quick release until all pressure is released.
5. Open and add marmalade. Stir.
6. Add cornstarch and water to thicken sauce.
7. Plate, top with green onions, and serve.

Tip: Serve orange chicken with a rice pilaf.

Meats

PICADILLO

Serves 4

Ingredients:

1½lbs ground beef
½ onion, chopped
2 cloves garlic, minced
1 tomato, chopped
1t sea salt
½ red bell pepper, chopped
½ can tomato sauce
2T cilantro
1t ground cumin
1 bay leaf
2T green olives
3T water

Instructions:

1. Set to "sear" and add ground beef and garlic. Brown the meat.
2. Add onions, tomatoes, sea salt, bell pepper, and cilantro. Sauté for 1 minute, and then add olives, cumin, and bay leaf.
3. Add tomato sauce and water. Mix well.
4. Close lid and lock. Set to "soup" for 15 minutes.
5. When done, quick release until all pressure is released. Open and remove bay leaf.

STUFFED FLANK STEAK

Serves 4

Ingredients:

- 3 strips of bacon
- 2 lbs flank steak
- 2 T horseradish
- 3 small pickles, halved lengthwise
- ½ c beef stock
- ½ c unsweetened apple juice
- 1 t dry thyme
- ¼ t ground cloves
- ¼ t freshly ground black pepper
- ½ T cornstarch

Instructions:

1. Set to "sear" and cook bacon. Remove bacon and place on cutting board.
2. Place steak on cutting board with the "flatter" side facing up. Smear horseradish over steak, and then alternate bacon and pickles down the steak.
3. Roll the flank steak, folding the bacon and pickles inside the steak.
4. Tie the steak with three pieces of butcher's twine.
5. Add broth, juice, thyme, cloves, and fresh ground pepper to pressure cooker.
6. Place steak in cooker.
7. Close lid and lock. Set to "meat/stew" and adjust for 60 minutes.
8. When done, natural release for 35 minutes. Afterward, quick release until all pressure is released.
9. Make a slurry out of water and cornstarch. Open cooker and add to the liquid in pot.
10. Remove steak. Slice. Spoon some sauce over the meat and serve.

PORK BELLY
WITH CHINESE SPICES

Serves 4

Ingredients:

- 1lb pork belly
- 2c white wine for cooking liquid, as needed
- Sea salt
- Freshly ground black pepper
- Oil (for searing)
- Chinese Five-Spice (optional)

Instructions:

1. Season pork belly with sea salt and fresh ground pepper (and/or season with Chinese "five-spice," optional).
2. Sear in oil, 2 to 3 minutes each side.
3. Pour in white wine.
4. Close lid and lock. Set to "meat/stew" and adjust for 40 minutes.
5. When done, natural release for 35 minutes. Afterward, quick release until all pressure is released.
6. Open. Remove pork belly.
7. When pork belly has reached room temperature, slice into equally sized portions. Sprinkle with sea salt.

Tip: To create a crispy crust, sear each side of pork belly in oil, 2-3 minutes per side.

Meats

LENGUA (BEEF TONGUE)
IN SALSA VERDE

Serves 6

Ingredients:

- 1 beef tongue, lightly rinsed
- ½ white onion, chopped
- 2 garlic cloves
- 1 bay leaf
- 2 sprigs of fresh thyme (or 1t dried thyme)
- 5c water

Salsa verde:

- 10 medium tomatillos
- 2 garlic cloves
- 3 serrano peppers (or 2 jalapeños)
- ½c chopped cilantro (reserve 1T for garnish)
- Sea salt and freshly ground pepper to taste
- 2T vegetable oil

Instructions:

1. Place the beef tongue in pressure cooker and add onions, garlic, bay leaf, and thyme. Cover with water.
2. Close lid and lock. Set to "meat/stew" for 40 minutes.
3. While meat is cooking, prepare salsa verde: Remove husks from tomatillos and rinse to remove sticky residue. Place tomatillos in a saucepan and add peppers and garlic.
4. Cover with water and bring to up a boil. Reduce heat to low and cook until tender, about 15 minutes.
5. When done, remove tomatillo mixture, allow to slightly cool, and place in a blender. Blend well.
6. Once meat is cooked, quick release until all pressure is released. Open, remove, and let cool.
7. Remove outer skin of meat. Cut meat into ½-inch slices.
8. Heat oil in a large skillet. Add salsa verde and season with sea salt and fresh ground pepper to taste.
9. Add meat slices to skillet and gently simmer for 8-10 minutes.
10. Garnish with chopped cilantro and remove bay leaf before serving.

SAUSAGE & PEPPERS

Serves 4

Ingredients:

- 2 pkg. Italian sausage
- 4 green bell peppers, cut into strips
- 1 can diced tomatoes
- 1 can tomato sauce
- 1c water
- 1T basil
- 3 cloves garlic, minced
- 1T Italian seasoning

Instructions:

1. Combine tomatoes, sauce, water, basil, garlic, and Italian seasoning in cooker.
2. Add sausage and place peppers on top.
3. Close lid and lock. Set to "poultry" and adjust for 25 minutes.
4. When done, quick release until all pressure is released.
5. Open and serve.

PULLED PORK CARNITAS

Serves 6

Ingredients:

2½lbs pork butt or pork shoulder, sliced into ¾-inch cubes
1 large onion, roughly chopped
2c low-sodium chicken broth (or more to cover meat)
½t cumin
1t dried chipotle powder

Instructions:

1. Put all ingredients into pressure cooker and stir.
2. Close lid and lock. Set to "meat/stew" and adjust for 35-45 minutes.
3. When done, quick release until all pressure is released.
4. Open. Drain and reserve the liquid.
5. Place pork on a plate and shred.
6. Put meat in a flat roasting pan and oven-broil for about 15 minutes, stirring often and adding juice from the pressure cooker.

Tip: Serve with tortillas, pico de gallo, rice, guacamole, lettuce, and cheese.

Meats

YANKEE POT ROAST
WITH MUSHROOMS

Serves 4

Ingredients:

- 1 (3- to 4-lb) boneless beef chuck-eye roast, trimmed
- Sea salt and freshly ground black pepper
- 1T vegetable oil
- 1 onion, finely chopped
- 2T tomato paste
- ½oz mushrooms, rinsed, quartered
- 2c beef broth
- 2lbs small Yukon Gold potatoes (1 to 3 inches in size for each)
- 2c carrots, sliced

Instructions:

1. Pat dry beef with paper towels and season with sea salt and fresh ground black pepper.
2. Set to "sear" and add oil.
3. When oil is hot, add beef and brown on all sides, 8-10 minutes. Remove beef to a platter.
4. Add onions and sauté for 3-5 minutes, stirring occasionally until soft.
5. Stir in tomato paste and mushrooms and cook about 3 minutes, stirring constantly.
6. Stir in broth and simmer for about 3 minutes until slightly reduced. Scrape up brown bits stuck on bottom of pressure cooker while broth is simmering and stir.
7. Return pot roast and any accumulated juices to pressure cooker.
8. Place potatoes and carrots on top of roast.
9. Close lid and lock. Set to "meat/stew" and adjust for 90 minutes.
10. When done, natural release for about 15 minutes.
11. Afterward, quick release until all pressure is released.
12. Open. Remove potatoes and beef to serving dishes.
13. Tent beef loosely with aluminum foil and let rest for 15 minutes before carving. Cover potatoes to keep warm.

Tip: While beef is resting, strain juices left in cooker and skim excess fat to make a gravy.

Meats

PORK SHANKS
WITH BEER & FENNEL SEEDS

Serves 2

Ingredients:

- 2 pork shanks (or hocks), cut in half
- Flour, for dredging, seasoned with sea salt and freshly ground black pepper
- 4T margarine
- 1 medium onion, diced
- 1 celery stalk, sliced or diced
- 2 carrots, peeled, chopped
- 3 large garlic cloves, chopped
- 2 bay leaves
- 2t dried thyme
- ½ can consommé
- 1 large can tomatoes, drained
- 1c beer
- 2t fennel seeds

Instructions:

1. Set to "sear" and add margarine.
2. Dredge pork in seasoned flour and add to cooker.
3. Brown pork on all sides; set aside.
4. Add onions, celery, carrots, garlic, bay leaves, fennel seeds, and thyme and sauté until soft.
5. Add beer and simmer for 5-10 minutes.
6. Add consommé and tomatoes.
7. Return pork to pressure cooker.
8. Close lid and lock. Set to "meat/stew" and adjust for 50 minutes.
9. When done, quick release until all pressure is released.
10. Open. Remove bay leaves. Serve.

Meats

SLOW-COOKED BUFFALO CHICKEN WINGS

Serves 4

Ingredients:

- 2lbs chicken wings, cut at the joint to make 24 pieces
- 1lb celery (garnish)
- 1c water

Coating:

- 4T hot sauce
- ¼c honey
- ¼c tomato puree
- 3t sea salt

Instructions:

1. Add water to pressure cooker. Place rack on the bottom.
2. Place chicken wings, evenly spaced, on rack.
3. Close lid and lock. Set to "poultry" and adjust for 10 minutes.
4. While chicken is cooking, in a bowl, add hot sauce, honey, tomato puree, and sea salt. Mix well with a fork until honey has completely dissolved.
5. When cooking is done, quick release until all pressure is released.
6. Open and remove wings and place into bowl with sauce. Toss to coat evenly.
7. Place chicken wings on parchment-covered paper.
8. Slide wings into a conventional oven and broil until brown and crispy, about 5 minutes.
9. Brush any remaining sauce onto chicken wings.
10. Serve on a platter with celery sticks and favorite dipping sauce.

Meats

SLOW-BRAISED BRISKET
WITH BBQ SAUCE

Serves 4

Ingredients:

- 3 lbs beef brisket, flat cut
- 1 t seasoned meat tenderizer
- ¼ t celery salt
- ¼ t seasoned salt
- ¼ t garlic salt
- 2 T liquid smoke
- 1 T Worcestershire sauce
- ½ c water
- 1 c BBQ sauce, plus additional reserved for serving

Instructions:

1. Combine meat tenderizer, celery salt, seasoned salt, and garlic salt in a small bowl.
2. Rub spices on brisket and place seasoned meat in a large, heavy, storage bag. Add liquid smoke and Worcestershire sauce. Seal bag and put in the refrigerator to marinate overnight.
3. Pour water and 1c BBQ sauce in pressure cooker (reserve some sauce). Add brisket (fat side up) with any juices left over from the marinating bag.
4. Close lid and lock. Set to "meat/stew" and adjust for 60 minutes.
5. When done, natural release, 15 minutes.
6. Afterward, quick release until all pressure is released.
7. Open and remove meat. Place brisket on a large platter or cutting board. Allow meat to rest for 5 minutes.
8. Mix reserved BBQ sauce with some of the cooking liquid.
9. Slice meat across the grain. Serve with BBQ sauce.

SOUTHERN-STYLE SMOTHERED CHICKEN

Serves 2

Ingredients:

- 1 lb chicken legs and thighs
- 1 c all-purpose flour
- 1 t celery seed
- 1 t onion powder
- 1 t poultry seasoning
- 1 t garlic powder
- 1 t smoked paprika
- ¼ c vegetable oil
- 2 c chicken broth
- 1 c whole milk
- 2 t garlic, minced
- 1 medium-sized onion, small dice
- Freshly ground black pepper

Instructions:

1. In a bowl, mix flour, celery seed, onion powder, poultry seasoning, garlic powder, and paprika.
2. Pat dry chicken and coat with the flour mixture; set aside.
3. In pressure cooker, set to "sear" and add oil.
4. When oil is hot, place chicken in (cook in batches). Cook each batch until golden brown on the outside. Remove chicken; set aside.
5. Add onions and garlic and sauté until golden brown.
6. Add 2T of the flour. Cook, moving the flour around with a whisk to eliminate lumps. Pour in chicken broth and milk. Continue whisking until there are no lumps.
7. Return all chicken pieces to cooker and into the liquid.
8. Close lid and lock. Set to "poultry" and adjust for 8 minutes.
9. When done, quick release until all pressure is released.
10. Open and check several chicken pieces with a meat thermometer. Internal temperature should be "165°F" or above.

Meats

PORK CHOPS IN BUTTERMILK SAUCE

Serves 4

Ingredients:

4	pork chops, each ¾ inches thick, bone-in
1c	all-purpose flour
2T	onion powder
2T	garlic powder
1t	sea salt
1t	cayenne pepper
½t	freshly ground black pepper
¼c	olive oil
1c	chicken broth
½c	buttermilk
	Flat-leaf parsley (for garnish)
1	green onion, sliced (for garnish)

Instructions:

1. Put flour in a shallow platter, and add onion powder, garlic powder, cayenne, salt, and fresh ground pepper. Mix well.
2. Pat dry pork chops, dredge in seasoned flour, and shake off excess. Set any leftover seasoned flour aside.
3. Set to "sear" and add oil.
4. When oil is hot, place pork chops in pressure cooker in a single layer. Fry 3-4 minutes each side until golden brown. Remove pork chops; set aside.
5. Add 2T of the leftover seasoned flour into the pan and the drippings from the chops. Mix flour into the fat to dissolve.
6. Pour in chicken broth.
7. Set to "sear" for 5 minutes to reduce and slightly thicken sauce. More time may be needed.
8. Whisk in buttermilk to make a creamy consistency to the sauce.
9. Return pork to cooker and coat the chops with sauce.
10. With the lid off, set to "sear" and simmer for 5 minutes until pork is cooked.
11. When pork is done, season with sea salt and fresh ground pepper to taste. Garnish with parsley and green onions. Serve.

Meats

SUGO MAILLE
(BRAISED PORK SAUCE)

Serves 4

Ingredients:

- 1½ lbs boneless pork center loin (or pork shoulder), cut into 1-inch cubes
- 1 small yellow onion, finely diced
- 3 carrots, finely diced
- 4 garlic cloves, minced
- 2t olive oil
- 2c red wine
- 1 (28-oz) can whole, peeled tomatoes
- 1T tomato paste
- ½t crushed red pepper flakes
- 1t dried oregano
- Coarse sea salt
- Peas (optional)

Instructions:

1. Set to "sear" and add olive oil.
2. Add pork and sear for 5 minutes until meat is browned on all sides.
3. Add remaining ingredients.
4. Close lid and lock. Set to "meat/stew" and adjust for 20 minutes.
5. When done, quick release until all pressure is released.
6. Open and remove inner pot. Break meat apart with 2 forks or with a potato masher.
7. Add sea salt and fresh ground pepper to taste.
8. Serve over pasta or polenta.

Meats

TRI-TIP BEEF IN MUSHROOM RED WINE SAUCE

Serves 4

Ingredients:

1 tri-tip roast
2 carrots, peeled, small dice
1 onion, small dice
1 pkg. mushrooms, cleaned, small dice
1-2 garlic cloves, peeled, minced
¼c butter
¾c red wine
    Sea salt
    Freshly ground black pepper
    Broccoli (optional)
    Potatoes (optional)

Instructions:

1. Set to "sear" and add meat. Sear meat on each side. Remove from cooker; set aside.
2. Place in mushrooms, vegetables, butter, and sauté.
3. Return beef to cooker. Pour in red wine.
4. Close lid and lock. Set to "meat/stew" and adjust for 17 minutes (for medium-rare).
5. When done, quick release until all pressure is released.
6. Open and add sea salt and fresh ground pepper to taste.

Meats

STOUT BEER BBQ RIBS

Serves 4

Ingredients:

- 2 racks baby back ribs, 1½ to 2 lbs each
- 1T vegetable, olive, or bacon oil
- 1 large onion, diced
- 4 garlic cloves, minced

Dry Rub:

- 2T smoked paprika
- 2T brown sugar
- 1½T chili powder
- 1t kosher salt
- ½t freshly ground black pepper

BBQ Sauce:

- 1½c ketchup
- 3T brown sugar
- 3T Worcestershire sauce
- 3T apple cider vinegar
- 1t dry mustard powder
- ¾t kosher salt
- 1c stout beer

Instructions:

1. Combine all dry rub ingredients. Sprinkle over ribs and rub into both sides of meat; set ribs aside.
2. Slice meat into two-rib sections and lay out on a large baking sheet lined with foil.
3. In a mixing bowl, whisk ketchup, brown sugar, Worcestershire sauce, apple cider vinegar, stout beer, mustard powder, and salt.
4. Set to "sear" and add oil. When oil is hot, add onions. Sauté onions for 3-4 minutes.
5. Add garlic and sauté for an additional 30 seconds, stirring often.
6. Add BBQ sauce from bowl into the cooker and stir.
7. Add a few ribs at a time, using tongs to gently coat them in sauce.
8. Arrange ribs standing upright with meat-side facing outward.
9. Close lid and lock. Set to "meat/stew" and adjust for 30 minutes.
10. When done, natural release for 15 minutes.
11. Afterward, quick release until all pressure is released.
12. Open and remove ribs, place on a platter, and coat with sauce.

Tip: (Optional) Arrange cooked ribs meat-side up on a baking sheet and broil shortly for a charred exterior.

TURKEY OSSO BUCO
WITH ONIONS & TOMATOES

Serves 6

Ingredients:

- 2 whole turkey legs, cut at joints into the drumstick and thigh, skin removed
- 1t dried thyme
- 1T olive oil
- 2 medium onions, small dice
- 2 medium carrots, peeled, small dice
- 2 celery stalks, small dice
- 6 cloves of garlic, minced and divided (¾, and ¼ for gremolata)
- ½c dry red wine
- 1 (28-oz) can diced tomatoes, with juice
- Sea salt
- Freshly ground black pepper

Gremolata:

- ¼c fresh Italian parsley, finely chopped
- 1t grated lemon peel
- ¼ (of the divided minced garlic)

Instructions:

1. Rub thyme on turkey and then season with sea salt and fresh ground black pepper; set aside.
2. Set to "sear" and add oil.
3. Add onions, carrots, and celery and sauté for about 8 minutes, stirring occasionally.
4. Add ¾ of the minced garlic. Pour in wine and add the turkey.
5. Let liquid reduce by about one-third, and then add tomatoes.
6. Close lid and lock. Set to "poultry" and adjust for 15 minutes.
7. When done, quick release until all pressure is released.
8. Open. Meat should be tender and fall off the bone.
9. Remove turkey and take meat off the bones.
10. Place meat back into the cooker and coat with the sauce.
11. In a small bowl, make the gremolata, mixing parsley, grated lemon peel, and remaining ¼ minced garlic. Mix well.
12. Serve braised turkey osso buco with gremolata spooned on top or on the side.

Meats

VEAL BLANQUETTE

Serves 4

Ingredients:

- 1 (2¼-lb) veal shoulder, cut into medium-sized pieces
- 1 veal tail (optional)
- 3 carrots, sliced
- 1 large leek, sliced
- ½ stick (¼c) butter
- ¼c flour
- 3 egg yolks
- 3¼fl oz heavy cream
- 1 bouquet garni (parsley, thyme, bay leaf, rosemary)
- 1 onion, peeled, studded with cloves
- Sea salt
- Freshly ground black pepper
- Mushrooms (optional)

Instructions:

1. Put veal into pressure cooker and cover with cold water.
2. Set to "sear" and bring up to a boil. Skim the top.
3. Add carrots, onion studded with cloves, leeks, bouquet garni, sea salt, and fresh ground pepper.
4. Close lid and lock. Set to "meat/stew" and adjust for 30 minutes.
5. While cooking, in a sauté pan, make a roux with the butter and flour, whisking well.
6. When veal is cooked, quick release until all pressure is released.
7. Open and remove meat.
8. Spoon cooking juice into the roux in pan, whisking well until smooth and thick, about 10 minutes.
9. Beat egg yolks and add to the roux. Add cream and combine. Pour roux into pressure cooker.
10. Return veal to sauce in cooker. Do not boil. Stir for a few minutes.
11. Remove bouquet garni. Serve veal hot with rice.

Meats

SWEDISH MEATBALLS IN GRAVY

Serves 4

Ingredients:

1c	fresh breadcrumbs	½t	freshly ground black pepper
¼c	whole milk	¼t	ground nutmeg
2T	unsalted butter	¼t	sea salt
1	small yellow onion, peeled, small dice	2c	low-fat beef broth
1lb	ground pork	¼c	all-purpose flour
¾lb	ground beef	1T	Worcestershire sauce
2	large egg yolks, room temperature	¼c	sour cream
1t	granulated sugar		Fresh parsley for garnish, finely chopped
½t	ground allspice		

Instructions:

1. Combine breadcrumbs and milk in small mixing bowl. Stir until breadcrumbs are thoroughly moistened; set aside.
2. Set to "sear" and melt butter in pressure cooker. Add onions and sauté until golden brown, about 10 minutes.
3. Transfer cooked onions and liquid to a large bowl. Cook for 10 minutes.
4. Turn off pressure cooker and wipe out.
5. Stir breadcrumb mixture into cooked onions in the large bowl.
6. Add ground beef, ground pork, egg yolks, sugar, ground allspice, black pepper, nutmeg, and sea salt to breadcrumb mixture. Mix well.
7. With dry hands, form into 12 individual 2-inch-sized balls.
8. In cooker, combine beef broth, all-purpose flour, and Worcestershire sauce. Mix well.
9. Bring gravy to a boil, stirring often.
10. Using a tablespoon, place meatballs into gravy.
11. Close lid and lock. Set to "time" and adjust for 8 minutes.
12. When done, quick release until all pressure is released.
13. Open. Using a slotted spoon, transfer cooked meatballs to a large bowl.
14. Stir sour cream into sauce, turn off cooker, and return meatballs to cooker. Cover for 5 minutes.
15. Sprinkle with fresh parsley and serve immediately.

Meats

VEAL OSSO BUCO

Serves 4

Ingredients:

- 4 (8½-oz) veal shanks, trimmed and tied (around each with kitchen twine to keep meat secured to bone)
- Sea salt and freshly ground black pepper
- 2T extra-virgin olive oil
- 2T red wine vinegar
- 1c red wine
- 1c onions, small dice
- 1c carrots, small dice
- 1c celery, small dice
- 1T fresh garlic, minced
- 1T tomato paste
- 3c beef stock
- 1 bay leaf
- 1 sprig of fresh rosemary

Instructions:

1. Set to "sear" and add oil.
2. When oil is hot, place veal shanks in and brown on both sides. Remove veal to a plate; set aside.
3. Add vegetables and sauté until they start to brown.
4. Add garlic and tomato paste. Stir until tomato paste begins to turn brown.
5. Deglaze the bottom with red wine vinegar and wine.
6. Return veal back to cooker and cover with beef broth, bay leaf, and rosemary.
7. Set to "meat/stew" and adjust for 1 hour.
8. When done, quick release until all pressure is released.
9. Open. Remove bay leaf. Remove meat. Cut twine off shanks and serve.

Meats

WHOLE BRAISED CHICKEN
WITH SRIRACHA

Serves 6

Ingredients:

- 3-lb whole chicken
- ¾c honey
- ¼c Sriracha
- ¾c soy sauce
- 1t garlic, minced
- 2T water
- 2T cornstarch
- 1T fresh basil, chopped
- Sea salt
- Freshly ground black pepper
- Jalapeño peppers (optional)

Instructions:

1. Set to "sear" and add oil.
2. Heavily season the chicken with sea salt and fresh ground black pepper, inside and outside of the bird.
3. Place chicken in pressure cooker and sear on all sides.
4. Add garlic, Sriracha, soy sauce, and honey.
5. Close lid and lock. Set to "poultry" and adjust for 25 minutes.
6. When done, quick release until all pressure is released.
7. Open carefully and remove chicken. Place on a platter to rest; set aside.
8. Leave liquid in pressure cooker. Set to "sear" and bring up to a boil.
9. In a small bowl, dissolve cornstarch in the 2T water. Add cornstarch mixture to cooker and stir. Continue to boil until sauce thickens.
10. Add basil and pour sauce over the chicken on the platter, or serve sauce on the side.

YANKEE POT ROAST
WITH CIDER

Serves 6

Ingredients:

- 1 (4-lb) boneless chuck roast
- 2T canola oil
- 1 large onion, medium dice
- 2 large carrots, medium dice
- 4 ribs of celery, medium dice
- 2T apple cider vinegar
- 2c apple cider
- 1qt beef stock
- Sea salt and freshly ground pepper
- 1 sprig of fresh thyme
- 1 (16-oz) can crushed tomatoes
- 2 large russet potatoes, peeled, medium dice

Instructions:

1. Set to "sear" and add oil.
2. Place beef in cooker and brown on all sides. Remove and place on a plate.
3. Add vegetables to fat in bottom of cooker.
4. Add vinegar, cider, and stock. Return beef to cooker.
5. Close lid and lock. Set to "meat/stew" and adjust for 1½ hours.
6. When done, quick release until all pressure is released.
7. Open and remove roast. Loosely cover with foil and let rest for 5 minutes before shredding up with fork and serving.

Meats

CHICKEN BREASTS IN BALSAMIC-DIJON SAUCE

Serves 4

Ingredients:

- 3T oil
- 4lbs chicken breasts, boneless
- ⅓c balsamic vinegar
- 1 onion, diced
- 3T Dijon mustard
- 4 sprigs thyme
- 2c chicken stock
- 2 bunches of small carrots, tops cut off
- 1lb small red potatoes

Instructions:

1. Set to "sear" and add oil.
2. When oil is hot, add chicken and sear on both sides. Remove chicken and set aside. Add onions and cook in the drippings.
3. Add balsamic vinegar and cook for 4 minutes.
4. Add Dijon mustard and stir.
5. Pour in chicken stock, thyme, potatoes, carrots, and return chicken back to pot.
6. Close lid and lock. Set to "poultry" and adjust for 15 minutes.
7. When done, natural release for 35 minutes. Afterward, quick release until all pressure is released.
8. Open, remove meat, and cover with foil. Let meat rest for 5 minutes.
9. Slice, plate with potatoes and carrots, and serve.

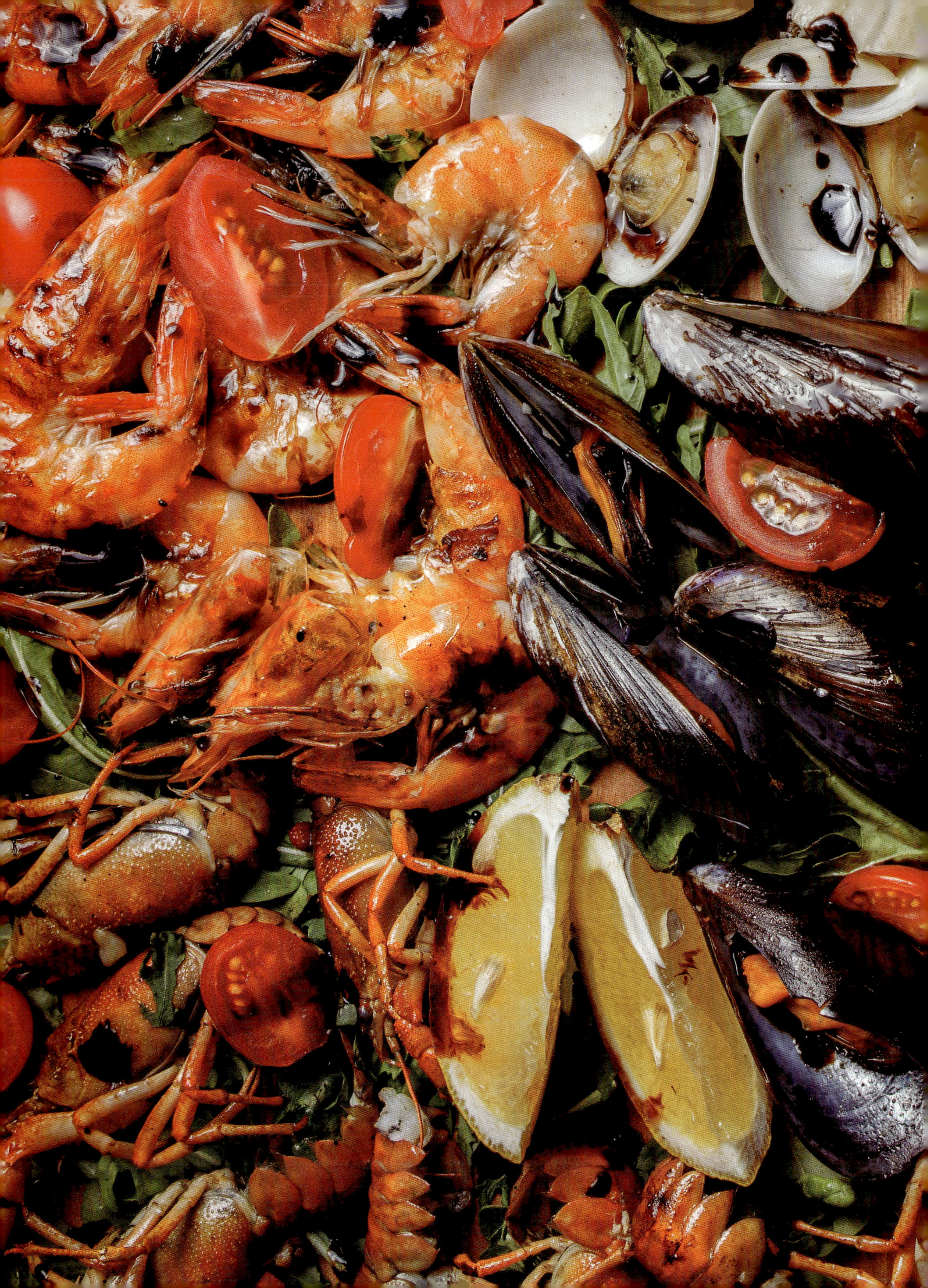

SEAFOOD

Cajun Shrimp Boil	190
Halibut Poached in Lemon & Butter	191
Bouillabaisse with Rouille Sauce	193
Mustard-Glazed Salmon with Chives	194
Portuguese Fish Stew	195
San Francisco Bay Cioppino	197
Rhode Island Steamed Clams	198
Salmon with Cilantro-Lime Adobo	199
Gulf Coast Seafood Gumbo	201
Sesame Steamed Mussels	202
Shrimp Creole	203
Spanish Seafood Paella	205
Swordfish, Nonna Gina Style	206
Tuscan-Style Shrimp Scampi	207

Seafood

CAJUN SHRIMP BOIL

Serves 4

Ingredients:

1½ lbs fresh shrimp, raw
12oz smoked sausage, cut into ¼-inch rounds
4 whole corn ears, each cut into three pieces
1lb red potatoes, skin on, cut into quarters
1 (12-oz) can beer
2 onions, cut into 8 large pieces
1T seafood seasoning
1t red chili pepper
8 cloves garlic, minced
Pinch of freshly ground black pepper
½t sea salt

Instructions:

1. Pour can of beer into pressure cooker.
2. Add the rest of the ingredients.
3. Close lid and lock. Set to "fish" and adjust for 6 to 8 minutes.
4. When done, quick release until all pressure is released.
5. Open and serve.

Seafood

HALIBUT POACHED IN LEMON & BUTTER

Serves 2

Ingredients:

- 2   (6-oz) halibut fillets (fresh)
- 2   sticks unsalted butter
- 2t blackening seasoning
- 1   lemon, cut into 8 slices
- 2T chopped parsley (for garnish)

Instructions:

1. Set to "sear", add butter to melt, and add lemon slices.
2. Season both sides of halibut fillets with seasoning and place on top of lemons in cooker.
3. Set to "fish" and adjust for 4 to 5 minutes.
4. When done, open and remove fish. Garnish with parsley.

Seafood

BOUILLABAISSE
WITH ROUILLE SAUCE

Serves 6

Ingredients:

3 lbs fish (3 different types; your choice, 1lb each)
8oz crabmeat
1lb whole clams
1lb mussels
2T olive oil
½ fennel bulb, sliced thin
2 leeks, sliced in half, white part only
2 cloves garlic, crushed
1c onions, sliced
4 Roma tomatoes, cut into 8 pieces
2t fresh thyme
1 bay leaf
½t saffron
2t sea salt
¼t freshly ground pepper
 Orange zest (from only one strip)
16oz fish stock or clam juice

Rouille Sauce:
1T fish broth
½c olive oil
1t freshly ground black pepper
2 garlic cloves
½t sea salt
¼c white bread, cubed, crusts removed

Instructions:

1. Set to "sear" and adjust for 10 minutes. Add olive oil, fennel, leeks, and onions and sauté.
2. Add garlic, tomatoes, bay leaf, thyme, saffron, and orange zest. Simmer for 10 minutes or until tomatoes are broken down.
3. Add fish stock or clam juice and seafood. Simmer for additional 10-12 minutes until mussels open and fish is cooked.
4. While bouillabaisse is cooking, make rouille sauce using a blender: Add 1T of the heated fish broth (stock) from the pressure cooker. Add garlic cloves, fresh ground black pepper, the ½t of sea salt, and bread cubes. Blend slowly, incorporating the olive oil to make a smooth paste.
5. When cooked, remove bouillabaisse with ladle and place into a serving bowl.
6. Top with some of the rouille sauce.

Seafood

MUSTARD-GLAZED SALMON
WITH CHIVES

Serves 4

Ingredients:

- 4 (6-oz) salmon steaks, skin on
- 1T Dijon mustard
- 1T lemon juice and zest
- Sea salt and freshly ground black pepper
- Fresh chives, chopped (for garnish)

Instructions:

1. In a bowl, mix lemon juice, zest, and Dijon mustard.
2. Sprinkle sea salt and fresh ground black pepper over salmon. Spread mustard mixture over the flesh side of the fish.
3. Set to "sear" and add oil.
4. When oil is hot, place salmon in skin side down.
5. Cook for 3 to 5 minutes or until skin is crispy.
6. Close lid and lock. Set to "fish" and adjust for 2-3 minutes.
7. When done, quick release until all pressure is released. Open lid carefully. Remove fish and garnish with chives.

Seafood

PORTUGUESE FISH STEW

Serves 4

Ingredients:

- 1lb raw large shrimp, peeled, deveined
- 1lb monkfish tails, cut into 2-inch pieces
- 4 large potatoes, peeled, medium dice
- 1 red bell pepper, sliced into ¼-inch moons
- 6 large plum tomatoes, large dice
- 1 medium yellow onion, small dice
- 2 cloves garlic, roughly chopped
- 1T tomato puree
- 1t paprika
- 1 bay leaf
- 1 pinch saffron
- 8oz dry white wine
- 2T olive oil
- ¼c chopped fresh parsley
- 2c fish stock

Instructions:

1. Set to "sear" and add olive oil.
2. When oil is hot, add onions, garlic, red bell peppers, and bay leaf and sauté for 5 minutes.
3. Add potatoes and plum tomatoes to the cooker.
4. In a bowl, mix white wine, fish stock, tomato puree, saffron, and paprika.
5. Add seafood to the cooker. Add mixture from bowl, covering seafood. Make sure all contents in cooker are covered (add more stock, if needed).
6. Close lid and lock. Set to "meat/stew" for 12 to 15 minutes.
7. When done, quick release until all pressure is released.
8. Open and garnish with parsley. Season with sea salt and fresh ground black pepper to taste.

Tip: Serve with crusty bread.

Seafood

SAN FRANCISCO BAY CIOPPINO

Serves 4

Ingredients:

- ⅓c   onions, small dice
- 3   garlic cloves, minced
- 1   green bell pepper, diced
- 1   red bell pepper, diced
- 1   celery stalk, diced
- 1   (28-oz) can plum tomatoes, small dice
- 1c   dry red wine or dry white wine
- 2T   fresh basil
- 1   bay leaf
- 1T   fresh parsley, finely chopped
- 2   (6-oz) cans clam meat
- 2c   clam juice
- 1lb   shrimp, peeled, deveined
- 1lb   scallops
- 1lb   whitefish (firm), cut into bite-sized pieces
- ¼c   olive oil

Instructions:

1. Set to "sear" and add olive oil, onions, and garlic. Sauté for 3 minutes.
2. Add bell peppers and celery and sauté for an additional 3 minutes.
3. Add plum tomatoes, wine, bay leaf, basil, and parsley.
4. Pour in clam juice and add chopped clams (with juice).
5. Place rest of seafood in cooker.
6. Close lid and lock. Set to "fish" and adjust for 8-10 minutes.
7. When done, quick release until all pressure is released.
8. Open carefully. Ladle into bowls.

Tip: Serve cioppino with crusty sourdough bread.

RHODE ISLAND STEAMED CLAMS

Serves 8

Ingredients:

- 4 lbs clams, cleaned, discard opened clams
- 1 onion, sliced in half
- ¼c parsley, chopped
- 2T fresh dill, chopped
- ¼c scallions, chopped
- ¼c olive oil
- 2c dry white wine
- 1t freshly ground black pepper

Instructions:

1. Place onion halves in and add olive oil.
2. Add clams and all herbs. Add white wine.
3. Close lid and lock. Set to "fish" for 8 minutes.
4. When done, quick release until all pressure is released.
5. Open carefully. Discard any clams that have not opened.

Seafood

SALMON
WITH CILANTRO-LIME ADOBO

Serves 2

Ingredients:

- 2 (5-oz) salmon steaks
- Sea salt and freshly ground black pepper
- 1T olive oil

Cilantro-lime adobo sauce:
- 1 (4-oz) can chipotle in adobo
- 2 cloves garlic, minced
- 1 lime (juice only)
- 1T agave
- 1T olive oil
- 1T hot water
- ½t paprika
- ½t cumin
- 1T cilantro, chopped

Instructions:

1. Open chipotle in adobo, and remove 2 peppers. Remove seeds and dice peppers small.
2. In a bowl, combine chipotle pepper, garlic, cilantro, olive oil, paprika, cumin, lime juice, agave, and hot water. Mix well; set adobo sauce aside.
3. Set to "sear" and add oil to pressure cooker.
4. Season salmon with sea salt and fresh ground pepper and place in cooker. Cook salmon for 2-3 minutes until salmon is done, flipping halfway.
5. Remove and drizzle adobo sauce over fish or serve on the side.

Seafood

GULF COAST SEAFOOD GUMBO

Serves 6

Ingredients:

- 2c smoked sausage, sliced
- 1lb crabmeat
- 24 shucked oysters
- 1lb shrimp, peeled, deveined
- 6c fish stock, divide 4c and 2c
- 1c onions, diced
- 4 celery stalks, small dice
- 2 red bell peppers, small dice
- 2T garlic, minced
- 2T fresh thyme
- ¼c parsley, finely chopped
- ¼c olive oil
- 1t sea salt
- ½t freshly ground pepper
- Cooked white rice
- ½c green onions, chopped

Roux:
- ¾c butter
- ¾c flour

Instructions:

1. Make a roux with flour and butter. Cook roux in a separate saucepan until it's a peanut butter color, approximately 10-15 minutes; set aside.
2. Set to "sear" and add oil to cooker. Add onions, celery, red bell peppers, and garlic and sauté for 5 minutes.
3. Add thyme and sausage. Cook for 5 minutes.
4. Add 4c of the fish stock into the pressure cooker.
5. Mix 2c of the fish stock in with the roux in the saucepan.
6. Add roux mixture to pressure cooker.
7. Continue cooking to thicken. Add shrimp, oysters, crabmeat, and chopped parsley.
8. Cook for an additional 2 to 3 minutes, or until shrimp and oysters are done.
9. Garnish with green onions. Serve gumbo with cooked white rice.

Tip: Do not leave roux unattended while cooking as it will easily burn. Stir very often.

Seafood

SESAME STEAMED MUSSELS

Serves 4

Ingredients:

- 2 lbs mussels, cleaned, beards removed (discard opened mussels)
- 1 T sesame seeds
- ½ c onions, small dice
- 2 jalapeños, seeds removed, small dice
- 2 cloves garlic, minced
- 2 T red chili flakes
- ¼ c olive oil
- ¼ c balsamic vinegar
- ¼ c dry white wine
- ½ c fresh basil, chopped
- 1 (28-oz) can crushed tomatoes
- 1 lemon, cut into wedges

Instructions:

1. Set to "sear" and add tomatoes, jalapeños, onions, sesame seeds, white wine, vinegar, olive oil, red chili flakes, and garlic. Bring up to a boil.
2. Add mussels and basil.
3. Close lid and lock. Set to "steam/veggies" and adjust for 5 minutes.
4. When done, quick release until all pressure is released. Open and squeeze lemon juice onto mussels, catching the seeds. Discard any unopened shellfish. Garnish mussels with the wedges.

Tip: Serve with toasted sourdough bread.

Seafood

SHRIMP CREOLE

Serves 4

Ingredients:

- 2 lbs medium shrimp, peeled, deveined
- 2 T vegetable oil
- 1 c green bell pepper, diced
- 1 c yellow onions, diced
- 2 celery stalks, small dice
- 4 garlic cloves, minced
- 2 t fresh thyme, finely chopped
- 1 t fresh oregano, finely chopped
- 1 t paprika
- 1 t Creole spice
- 1 c chicken broth
- 1 (14-oz) can diced tomatoes, with juice
- ½ c dry white wine
- 2 T tomato paste
- 1 T Worcestershire sauce
- 4 scallions, sliced thin

Instructions:

1. Set to "sear" and add vegetable oil. Add onions, bell peppers, celery, and garlic and sauté.
2. Add thyme, oregano, paprika, and Creole spice and cook for 1 minute.
3. Add tomato paste, white wine, Worcestershire sauce, diced tomatoes with juice, and chicken broth.
4. Close lid and lock. Set to "soup" and adjust for 10 minutes.
5. When done, quick release until all pressure is released.
6. Open lid carefully. Set cooker to "sear" and adjust for about 2-3 minutes. Add shrimp and cook until shrimp becomes opaque.

Seafood

SPANISH SEAFOOD PAELLA

Serves 4

Ingredients:

- 1c   green bell peppers, diced
- 1c   red bell peppers, diced
- 1c   onions, diced
- 2c   short-grain rice, uncooked
- 4T   olive oil
- 2t   sea salt
- ½t   saffron
- ⅛t   ground turmeric
- 1¾c vegetable stock
- 1   bay leaf
- 1c   firm whitefish (your choice), cut up into medium-sized cubes
- ½lb clams
- ½lb shrimp
- ½lb mussels

Instructions:

1. Set to "sear" and add olive oil, onions, and bell peppers. Sauté for 3 to 4 minutes.
2. Add rice and saffron to cooker. Set for an additional 2 minutes.
3. When done, add all seafood and pour in stock. Add turmeric, sea salt, and bay leaf.
4. Close lid and lock. Set to "fish" and adjust for 12 minutes.
5. When done, natural release, 2 minutes.
6. Afterward, quick release until all pressure is released.
7. Open and remove bay leaf. Gently stir, mixing the paella. Serve.

Seafood

SWORDFISH, NONNA GINA STYLE

Serves 4

Ingredients:

- 2T olive oil
- 2 swordfish steaks, boneless
- ½t salt
- 1 onion, small dice
- 1T garlic, minced
- 1 (14-oz) can diced tomatoes
- ½c chicken broth
- ½c clam juice
- 2t red wine vinegar
- Parsley, chopped

Instructions:

1. Set to "sear" and add olive oil.
2. Season the swordfish and place in the hot oil, browning both sides, about 4 minutes per side.
3. Remove swordfish.
4. Add garlic and onions to oil in cooker.
5. Pour in tomatoes, broth, clam juice, and red wine vinegar.
6. Close lid and lock. Set to "time" and adjust for 5 minutes.
7. When done, quick release until all pressure is released.
8. Open. Return swordfish steaks to pressure cooker.
9. Close lid and lock. Set to "fish" and adjust for 3 minutes.
10. When done, quick release until all pressure is released.
11. Open. Remove fish and garnish with chopped parsley. Serve.

Seafood

TUSCAN-STYLE SHRIMP SCAMPI

Serves 4

Ingredients:

- 1lb shrimp, shelled, deveined, raw
- 2T   lemon juice
- ½c   dry white wine
- 1T   fresh garlic, minced
- 2T   unsalted butter
- 2T   fresh parsley, chopped
- 2T   olive oil
- 1   pinch red chili flakes (optional)
- 8oz cooked linguine

Instructions:

1. Cook the pasta as directed on package; set aside.
2. Set to "sear" and add butter and olive oil. Add in garlic and red chili flakes (optional) and sauté for 1 minute.
3. Pour in lemon juice and white wine.
4. Add shrimp and cook for 2 minutes or until all are opaque and done.
5. Stir in precooked pasta and parsley. Serve.

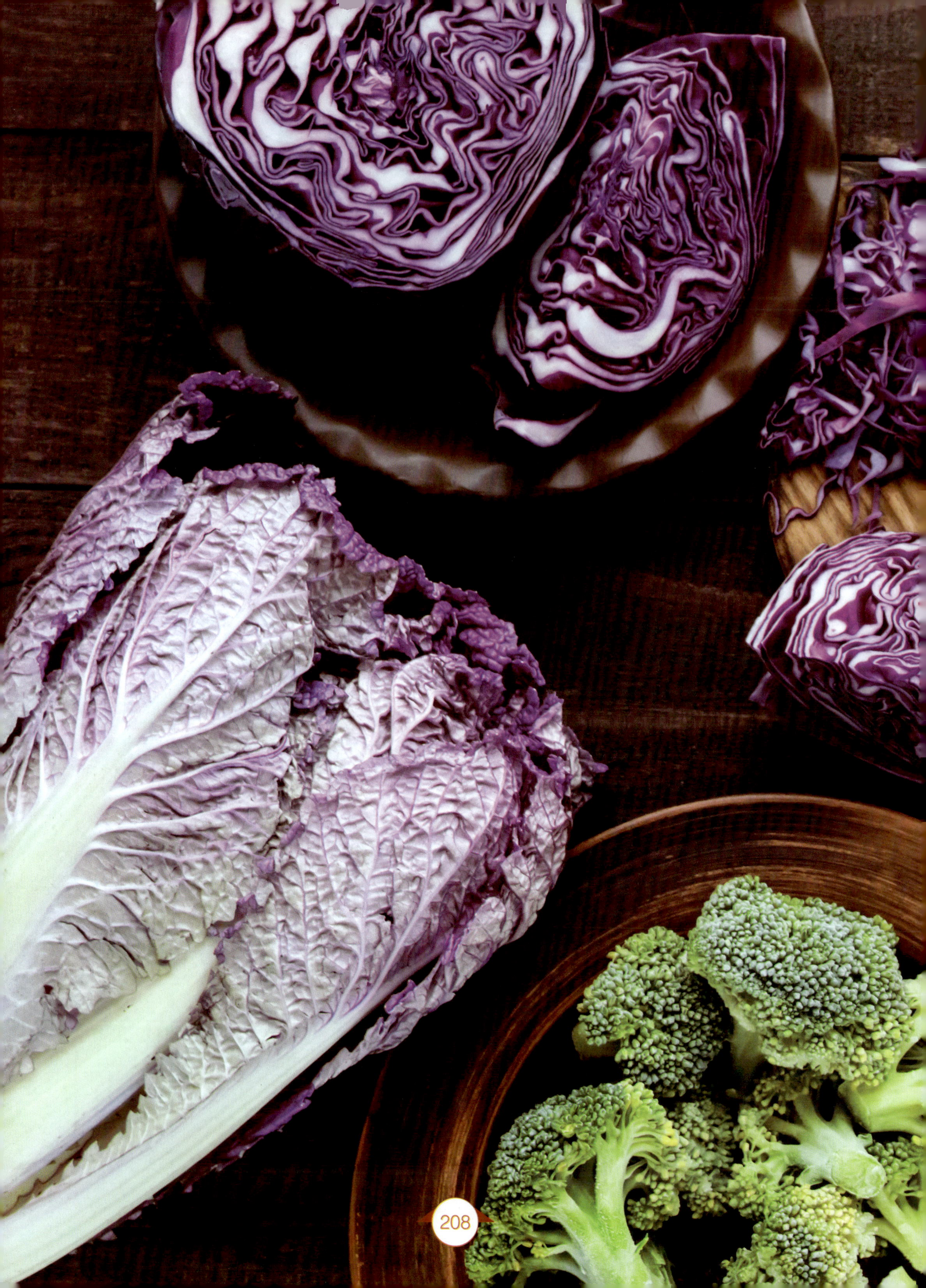

VEGETABLES & SIDES

Baked Potatoes 210
Boston Baked Beans 211
Braised Red Cabbage with
Vinegar & Red Wine 213
Braised Beets with
Pickling Spices 214
Cheesy Potatoes Au Gratin 215
Chickpea Madras Curry 217
Corn on the Cob 218
Cornbread 219
Crustless Cuban Egg Quiche .. 221
Diced Potatoes 222
Eggplant & Squash
Ratatouille 223
Pozole Verde 225
Fresh Sage Spaghetti Squash 226
Fried Rice 227
Real Butter Mashed Potatoes .. 229
Glazed Root Vegetables 230
Honey-Glazed Carrots
with Almonds 231

Warm German Potato Salad 233
Kale with Lemon, Garlic,
& Poppy Seeds 234
Marsala Mushrooms 235
New England-Style
Creamed Corn 236
Oatmeal 237
Quinoa & Veggies 238
Quinoa Tabbouleh 239
Quinoa 240
Soft- or Hard-Boiled Eggs 241
Southern Greens
with Smoked Bacon 242
Steamed Sweet Potatoes with
Agave Nectar & Sea Salt 243
Sweet Acorn Squash 244
Sweet & Spicy Cabbage
with Caraway 245
Sweet Potatoes with Pecans
& Bourbon 246
Whole Baby Potatoes 247

Vegetables & Sides

BAKED POTATOES

Serves 4

Ingredients:

4 to 8 medium-sized russet potatoes, cleaned
Sea salt
Freshly ground black pepper
1c water
Butter (optional)

Instructions:

1. Poke holes throughout the potatoes with a fork.
2. Pour in water and add rack to bottom of pressure cooker. Place potatoes on top of rack.
3. Close lid and lock. Set to "potatoes" and adjust for 12 minutes.
4. When done, natural release, 10 minutes.
5. Afterward, quick release until all pressure is released.
6. Open lid carefully. Remove potatoes. Open each with a knife or squeeze to let steam come out more at top. Add sea salt, fresh ground black pepper, and butter (optional). Serve.

Vegetables & Sides

BOSTON BAKED BEANS

Serves 10

Ingredients:

- 1lb dried navy beans
- ½lb thick, smoked bacon, cut into ½-inch pieces
- 1 large onion, diced
- 1 carrot, peeled, diced
- 2 cloves of garlic, minced
- 1 bay leaf
- 1 sprig of thyme
- 1 sprig of sage
- 2t Dijon mustard
- ½c dark molasses
- ½c ketchup
- ¼c brown sugar
- 8c water, to soak
- 2½c water
- Sea salt and freshly ground black pepper

Instructions:

1. Rinse beans well. If possible, soak overnight in pressure cooker or other container with 8c water and 1T sea salt.
2. When ready to cook, drain and rinse beans and discard soaking liquid.
3. Set to "sear" and add bacon.
4. When bacon is cooked, take out and drain on paper towel. Leave bacon fat in cooker.
5. Add onions, carrot, and garlic to bacon fat and cook for 3 minutes.
6. Add the 2½c water, molasses, ketchup, brown sugar, mustard, bay leaf, thyme, sage, sea salt, fresh ground black pepper, bacon, and beans. Stir well.
7. Close and lock lid. Set to "beans" and adjust for 35 minutes.
8. When done, quick release until all pressure is released.
9. Open and check to see if beans are fully cooked (additional 5 to 10 minutes may be needed).
10. Add sea salt and fresh ground black pepper to taste, if needed. Remove bay leaf before serving. Serve hot.

Vegetables & Sides

BRAISED RED CABBAGE
WITH VINEGAR & RED WINE

Serves 4

Ingredients:

2½lbs red cabbage
1 large onion, diced
2 large green apples, peeled, cored, and finely diced
¼c red wine vinegar
1c red wine
3 bay leaves
1c beef broth
1t salt
¼t black pepper
¼t ground cloves
1 cinnamon stick
3T brown sugar
1T cornstarch
2T unsalted butter (bacon fat)
2T red currant jam (optional)

Instructions:

1. In a bowl, dissolve cornstarch with 2T of the red wine, plus 1T of the red wine vinegar; set aside.
2. Remove outer leaves of the cabbage and discard.
3. Cut cabbage into ½-inch strips or use a food processor with a slicing disk, or use a mandoline slicer; set aside.
4. Set to "sear" and add butter.
5. Once melted, add onions and apples and sauté until soft, about 10 minutes.
6. Add cabbage in, mixing well.
7. Add in remaining red wine vinegar and red wine, beef broth, bay leaves, ground cloves, brown sugar, cinnamon stick, sea salt, and fresh ground black pepper.
8. Close lid and lock. Set to "steam/veggies" and adjust for 8 minutes.
9. When done, quick release until all pressure is released.
10. Open lid and pour reserved red wine and cornstarch mixture from bowl over the cabbage. Add red currant jam (optional).
11. Mix well, set cooker to "sear", and bring to a boil until liquid with cabbage thickens.

Vegetables & Sides

BRAISED BEETS
WITH PICKLING SPICES

Serves 4

Ingredients:

6	medium beets
2c	water
2T	mustard seeds
1T	whole allspice
2t	coriander seeds
2	whole cloves
1t	ground ginger
1t	crushed red pepper flakes
1	bay leaf, crumbled
1	cinnamon stick
½c	apple cider vinegar

Instructions:

1. Wash and trim ends of beets. Keep them whole; do not cut in half.
2. In the pressure cooker, add water, vinegar, and spices.
3. Arrange beets in the pickling water.
4. Close lid and lock. Set to "beans" and adjust for 15 minutes. (Size of beets: if beets are smaller, cooking time may be 10 minutes; if beets are larger, time may be 15-20 minutes.)
5. After cooking, quick release until all pressure is released.
6. Open and check to see if beets are done. If so, let them cool down in the pickling liquid.
7. Once cooled, remove bay leaf. Remove beets, peel, and cut into quarters or 1-inch pieces.

Tip: You can preserve your beets in the pickling solution. And when serving them, you can drain them and then drizzle olive oil on top.

Vegetables & Sides

CHEESY POTATOES AU GRATIN

Serves 6

Ingredients:

- 6 medium potatoes, peeled, sliced into ⅛-inch-thick slices
- 2T butter
- 1c chicken broth
- ½c onions, small dice
- ½c sour cream
- 1c shredded Monterey Jack cheese
- Sea salt
- Freshly ground black pepper

For topping:
- 3T butter
- 1c panko breadcrumbs

Instructions:

1. Set to "sear" and add butter. When melted, add onions and sauté until tender, about 5 minutes.
2. Add chicken broth. Add sea salt and fresh ground black pepper.
3. Place the steamer rack in bottom of cooker. Place sliced potatoes on top.
4. Close lid and lock. Set to "potatoes" and adjust for 5 minutes.
5. When done, quick release until all pressure is released.
6. Open and remove steam rack with potatoes; save the liquid.
7. Arrange potatoes in a greased 9x13 baking dish.
8. In a bowl, add liquid from the pressure cooker, sour cream, and cheese. Mix well. Pour over potatoes.
9. In a bowl, mix panko breadcrumbs with 3T melted butter. Sprinkle on top of potatoes.
10. Broil in regular oven for 5 minutes or until golden brown.

Vegetables & Sides

CHICKPEA MADRAS CURRY

Serves 4

Ingredients:

- 2c dried chickpeas (garbanzo beans), soaked overnight, rinsed, drained
- 5c water
- 2T olive oil or ghee, divided
- 1 large yellow onion, small dice
- 1 green chili pepper, seeds and membrane removed, minced
- 1T fresh ginger, minced
- 3 Roma tomatoes, diced
- 3 cloves of garlic, minced
- 2T ketchup
- 4c chicken or vegetable broth
- 1t ground turmeric
- 1½t sea salt
- 2 bay leaves
- ¼c cilantro, chopped
- 1T whole coriander seeds
- 1T whole cumin seeds
- ½t green cardamom
- ½t fenugreek seeds
- ½t whole fennel seeds
- 1t whole black peppercorns
- 1 small, whole cinnamon stick

Instructions:

1. Add chickpeas, water, and 1t of the sea salt to cooker.
2. Close lid and lock. Set to "beans" and adjust for 45 minutes.
3. When done, quick release until all pressure is released.
4. Open and check to see if chickpeas are cooked. If not, close lid and cook for an additional 15 minutes. Once cooked, quick release until all pressure is released. Open and drain; set aside.
5. In a frying pan, add coriander seeds, cumin seeds, green cardamom, fenugreek seeds, fennel seeds, black peppercorns, and the cinnamon stick. Toast for 3 to 4 minutes or until very fragrant.
6. Remove from heat and cool completely.
7. Grind seeds in a spice grinder until they become a fine powder; set aside.
8. Set pressure cooker to "sear". Add 1T olive oil or ghee and add chickpeas in small batches. Brown chickpeas and add more oil as needed to finish; set aside.
9. Add remaining oil or ghee and add onions to cooker and cook 8-10 minutes until lightly browned.
10. Add ginger, garlic, and green chili. Cook for 2 minutes.
11. Add ground reserved spice mixture and turmeric. Cook for 1 minute.
12. Add tomatoes and ketchup and cook for 5 minutes.
13. Return chickpeas to cooker, add broth, sea salt, and bay leaves.
14. Set cooker to "sear" and cook 1 hour, stirring occasionally. Add more broth if curry gets too dry.
15. Add remaining sea salt to taste, stir in cilantro, and simmer for an additional 5 minutes. Serve with white rice.

Vegetables & Sides

CORN ON THE COB

Serves 8

Ingredients:

- 8 ears of corn
- 2c of water
- Butter
- Sea salt

Instructions:

1. Cut off the bottom (shank) of corn and remove husks and all corn silk. Wash well under water; set aside.
2. To the pressure cooker, add water and arrange ears of corn diagonally (if they don't fit, place them vertically with the thick part in the water to ensure even cooking).
3. Close lid and lock. Set to "beans" and adjust for 2 to 3 minutes.
4. When done, natural release for 35 minutes. Afterward, quick release until all pressure is released.
5. Open, remove corn with tongs, and serve with butter and sea salt.

Vegetables & Sides

CORNBREAD

Serves 6

Ingredients:

- 2 pkg. corn muffin mix
- 1c milk
- 2 eggs

Instructions:

1. In a bowl, add corn muffin mix, milk, and eggs. Mix well.
2. Pour batter into greased, 7-inch pan (to fit into cooker).
3. Pour 1c water into cooker and place rack on the bottom. Place pan on top of rack.
4. Close lid and lock. Set to "bake" and adjust for 20 minutes.
5. When done, natural release for 35 minutes. Afterward, quick release until all pressure is released.
6. Open and carefully remove pan. Let cornbread cool in pan for 5 minutes.
7. Remove cornbread from pan and place on a wire rack to continue to cool.

Vegetables & Sides

CRUSTLESS CUBAN EGG QUICHE

Serves 4

Ingredients:

- 6 large eggs
- 4oz frozen hash browns (or raw potatoes)
- 1T melted butter
- ¼c onions, diced
- 1 clove garlic, minced
- 2T baking mix
- ¼c milk
- 1t tomato paste
- 4oz grated cheese (your choice)
- 1oz grated cheese (your choice, for topping)
- 1½c water
- ½c green bell peppers, diced
- ½c bacon, diced
- 1c spinach, chopped
- ½c ham
- ½c sausage (your choice)

Instructions:

1. If using raw potatoes, peel and cut potatoes into thin slices and soak in water for 20 minutes; if using frozen potatoes, defrost before use.
2. In a medium bowl, whisk eggs and seasoning until frothy; set aside.
3. In a liquid mixing cup, whisk baking mix, tomato paste, and milk. Add to egg mixture (will give structure to eggs).
4. Add onions and garlic to mixture. Add vegetables, 4oz cheese, and meats.
5. Grease a round casserole dish (to fit in pressure cooker).
6. If using raw potatoes, drain water and pat dry. Add the potatoes to casserole dish and add melted butter. If using frozen potatoes, add potatoes to casserole dish with no butter.
7. Pour egg mixture over potatoes.
8. Place rack on bottom of pressure cooker and pour water in. Set the quiche on top of rack.
9. Close lid and lock. Set to "bake" and adjust for 15-20 minutes.
10. When done, natural release for 35 minutes. Afterward, quick release until all pressure is released.
11. Open and remove quiche. Top with grated cheese and serve.

Vegetables & Sides

DICED POTATOES

Serves 4

Ingredients:

- 1lb small potatoes, washed, peeled, diced (cut) into quarters or 1- to 1½-inch cubes
- 1c water
- 1t oil
- 3T butter
- Parsley, minced
- Sea salt
- Freshly ground black pepper

Instructions:

1. Pour water and oil into cooker.
2. Place rack on bottom. Place potatoes on rack.
3. Close lid and lock. Set to "potatoes" and adjust for 3 minutes.
4. When done, quick release until all pressure is released.
5. Open. Season potatoes with butter, sea salt, fresh ground pepper, and parsley. Serve.

Vegetables & Sides

EGGPLANT & SQUASH RATATOUILLE

Serves 6

Ingredients:

1½ lbs eggplant, peeled, medium dice
1 large green bell pepper, seeded, diced
1 large red bell pepper, seeded, diced
1 medium zucchini, medium dice
1 medium yellow squash, medium dice
1c onions, diced
2 cloves of garlic, minced
3T olive oil
½c water
1t dried thyme or oregano
1t sea salt
1 (14-oz) can diced tomatoes, with juice
1c basil, tightly packed, finely chopped
Pinch of sugar

Instructions:

1. Set to "sear" and add 2T of the olive oil.
2. When oil is hot, add onions, garlic, and bell peppers and sauté until cooked.
3. Add eggplant, yellow squash, and zucchini. Stir well to coat.
4. Add water, thyme, sugar, and sea salt. Mix.
5. Add the tomatoes on top, but DO NOT STIR.
6. Close lid and lock. Set to "steam/veggies" and adjust for 3 minutes.
7. When done, quick release until all pressure is released.
8. Open and add basil. Stir. Add the remaining olive oil (1T).

Tip: For a thicker consistency, puree 1c of the ratatouille and pour back in.

Vegetables & Sides

POZOLE VERDE

Serves 6

Ingredients:

2-lb pork shoulder butt, cut into 1½-inch cubes
      Sea salt
½c   pumpkin seeds
28oz tomatillos, drained
3   fresh poblano peppers, seeds, stems removed, small dice
1   small sprig cilantro
2 or 3 cloves garlic, minced
1   onion, chopped
      Sea salt
      Freshly ground black pepper
½c   chicken stock (optional, to puree)

3T   vegetable oil
1T   Mexican oregano
1t   cumin
2 or 3 red potatoes, diced
1   (36½-oz) can hominy, drained
2c   chicken stock

Garnish:

1   radish, thinly sliced
      Deep-fried corn tortilla strips
1   fresh lime, cut into wedges
1   red onion, sliced very thin
1   avocado, flesh removed, chopped

Instructions:

1. Set to "sear" and add 1T of the vegetable oil.
2. When hot, add salt to pork and place in and brown. Cook one batch at a time until all pork is done.
3. Remove pork to a bowl.
4. In a dry skillet, toast pumpkin seeds over medium heat until they swell up and start to pop. Remove seeds; set aside.
5. Cool pumpkin seeds down, put them in a blender or food processor, and grind to a fine powder.
6. In a food processor or blender, add tomatillos, peppers, salt, and fresh ground pepper, onion, garlic, and cilantro. Process until completely smooth. (Add up to ½c chicken stock if mixture is too thick to use in the food processor.)
7. Set cooker to "sear". Heat 2T (remaining) of the vegetable oil in the pressure cooker. Pour in the green pumpkin seed/tomatillo puree and simmer 15 to 25 minutes until the color deepens (mixture will thicken and color will become darker and richer).
8. Add pork, oregano, cumin, and chicken stock.
9. Close lid and lock. Set to "soup" and adjust for 20 minutes.
10. When done, quick release until all pressure is released.
11. Open and add in potatoes and the drained, rinsed hominy.
12. Close lid and lock. Set to "time" and adjust for 3 minutes.
13. When done, quick release until all pressure is released.
14. Open. Portion out into bowls or plates and top each with sliced radishes, tortilla strips, red onions, avocado, cilantro, and a lime wedge.

Vegetables & Sides

FRESH SAGE SPAGHETTI SQUASH

Serves 4

Ingredients:

3lbs spaghetti squash
1c water
2T fresh sage leaves
Sea salt and freshly ground black pepper

Instructions:

1. Wash squash well, cut off the stemmed end, and then cut in half, lengthwise. Carefully remove all seeds with a spoon.
2. Season squash with sea salt and fresh ground black pepper and sprinkle sage over top.
3. Place rack on the bottom of pressure cooker and add water. Place squash on rack flesh-side up.
4. Close lid and lock. Set to "steam/veggies" and adjust for 8 minutes.
5. When done, quick release until all pressure is released.
6. Open and remove. Allow squash to cool.
7. Using a fork, scrape the strands of spaghetti squash from the skin and place in a bowl.

Tip: Serve spaghetti squash with a marinara sauce. See "Marinara" recipe in Soups, Stews, & Sauces section.

Vegetables & Sides

FRIED RICE

Serves 4

Ingredients:

- 2c   rice
- 1T   oil
- 1t   sesame oil
- ½   onion, diced
- 1T   garlic, minced
- 2   scallions, sliced thin
- 1½c   water
- 1   carrot, diced
- 1½c   peas
- 3T   soy sauce
- 2   eggs
- 1c   cabbage, shredded
- 1c   bean sprouts

Instructions:

1. Set to "sear" and add oil.
2. When oil is hot, add onions and sauté until brown.
3. Pour in rice and toast, about 2 minutes. Add garlic and brown. Add water.
4. Add carrots, peas, and scallions.
5. Close lid and lock. Set to "steam/veggies" and adjust for 2 minutes.
6. When done, quick release until all pressure is released.
7. Open, set to "sear", and add in eggs and soy sauce. Scramble the eggs. Mix well.
8. Add cabbage and bean sprouts and cook until cabbage is wilted. Serve.

Vegetables & Sides

REAL BUTTER MASHED POTATOES

Serves 6

Ingredients:

2lbs russet potatoes, peeled, quartered
⅔c whole milk
8T   butter (1 stick), melted
1c   water
     Sea salt and freshly ground black pepper

Instructions:

1. Place rack in bottom of cooker. Place potatoes on rack and add water.
2. Close lid and lock. Set to "steam/veggies" and adjust for 7 minutes.
3. Once cooked, quick release pressure until all pressure is released.
4. Open and remove potatoes with the rack; set potatoes aside and discard any liquid.
5. Place potatoes in a bowl and whip with a hand mixer until smooth; set aside.
6. Add butter, whole milk, sea salt, and fresh ground black pepper to whipped potatoes, serve immediately.

Vegetables & Sides

GLAZED ROOT VEGETABLES

Serves 6

Ingredients:

- 2 medium turnips, peeled, cut into eighths
- 8oz baby carrots
- 2 medium parsnips, peeled, sliced into ½-inch pieces
- 2T sugar
- 2t ground ginger
- 1c chicken broth
- 1T cornstarch with ½c cold water (optional)
- 2T olive oil

Instructions:

1. Set to "sear" and add oil.
2. Add turnips, parsnips, and carrots and sauté for 3 to 5 minutes.
3. Add chicken broth, sugar, and ginger.
4. Close lid and lock. Set to "steam/veggies" and adjust for 3 minutes.
5. When done, quick release until all pressure is released.
6. Open lid carefully and serve.

Tip: Sauce in cooker can be thickened by combining cornstarch and water and stirring into the liquid. Set the cooker to "sear" and stir constantly until thick.

Vegetables & Sides

HONEY-GLAZED CARROTS
WITH ALMONDS

Serves 6

Ingredients:

- 1lb   baby carrots, washed, peeled
- 1c   water
- 2T   butter
- 1t   dried dill
- 1t   dried thyme
- ½c   honey
- ½c   slivered almonds
- Sea salt and freshly ground black pepper to taste

Instructions:

1. In the pressure cooker, place rack on bottom. Set carrots on top of rack. Pour in the water.
2. Close lid and lock. Set to "steam/veggies" and adjust for 3 minutes.
3. Once done, quick release until all pressure is released.
4. Open and take out carrots; set aside. Remove rack. Discard any liquid and wipe the pot clean.
5. Set to "sear" and add butter. When melted, add the dill and thyme and cook for 30 seconds or until very fragrant.
6. Add carrots, sea salt, fresh ground black pepper, almonds, and honey and sauté until well coated, about 5 minutes. Serve hot.

Tip: Serve with chicken or fish.

Vegetables & Sides

WARM GERMAN POTATO SALAD

Serves 6

Ingredients:

2 lbs red potatoes, cut into ½-inch chunks
6 slices thick-cut smoked bacon, diced into ½-inch pieces
1 onion, finely chopped
½c chicken broth
½c apple cider vinegar
1t Worcestershire sauce
1T grainy or Dijon mustard
½t celery seeds
1T sugar
3T flat-leaf parsley, finely chopped
Sea salt and freshly ground black pepper

Instructions:

1. Set cooker to "sear" and add bacon. Cook until bacon is crispy. Once crispy, remove bacon to paper towel and set aside to drain excess fat.
2. Add onions to bacon fat in cooker and sauté until translucent. Do not brown onions.
3. Remove onions and wipe cooking pot clean.
4. Place potatoes in pressure cooker and cover with water.
5. Close lid and lock. Set to "steam/veggies" and adjust for 7 minutes.
6. Once cooked, quick release until all pressure is released.
7. Open. Remove potatoes and drain. Discard the liquid.
8. Return potatoes to pressure cooker and add vinegar, broth, Worcestershire sauce, mustard, celery seeds, sugar, sea salt, and fresh ground black pepper.
9. Set to "sear". Bring it just up to a boil for 3 minutes. Most of liquid will be evaporated.
10. Mix in onions, bacon, and parsley.

Tip: Serve potato salad warm or cold.

Vegetables & Sides

KALE WITH LEMON, GARLIC, & POPPY SEEDS

Serves 4

Ingredients:

- 1 lb kale, cleaned, stems trimmed
- 3 cloves of garlic, sliced thin
- Juice of ½ lemon
- ½ c water
- 1 t poppy seeds
- 1 T olive oil
- Sea salt and freshly ground black pepper

Instructions:

1. Set to "sear" and add oil.
2. When oil is hot, add garlic and sauté. Do not let garlic brown.
3. Add a handful of kale and mix in with the garlic and oil. Continue adding more kale in, packing pressure cooker with as much as you want as long as lid can close; the kale will wilt quickly.
4. Sprinkle kale with sea salt and fresh ground black pepper. Pour water over kale.
5. Close lid and lock. Set to "steam/veggies" for 5 minutes.
6. When done, quick release until all pressure is released.
7. Open and squeeze lemon juice on top of kale and sprinkle on poppy seeds. Add more fresh ground pepper and sea salt to taste, if needed.
8. Scoop out kale, leaving behind as much liquid as possible.

Vegetables & Sides

MARSALA MUSHROOMS

Serves 4

Ingredients:

- 1 lb cremini mushrooms, cut in half
- ¼ c Marsala wine
- ½ red onion, small dice
- 6 cloves of garlic, minced
- ½ c vegetable stock or mushroom stock
- 2 T butter or olive oil
- Sea salt and freshly ground black pepper

Instructions:

1. Set to "sear" and add the butter and onions. Sauté until translucent.
2. Add garlic. When fragrant, add the mushrooms. Mix well.
3. Pour in Marsala wine. Bring up to a boil and add vegetable stock.
4. Close lid and lock. Set to "steam/veggies" and adjust for 1-2 minutes.
5. When done, quick release until all pressure is released.
6. Open and season with sea salt and fresh ground black pepper to taste.

Tip: Instead of using butter or olive oil, use 4 strips of bacon: Chop bacon, set to "sear", and cook until crispy. Pull out and set aside on paper towel. Leave 1 to 2T fat in bottom of cooker. Add next ingredients and return bacon to cooker with mushrooms before closing lid and cooking.

Vegetables & Sides

NEW ENGLAND-STYLE CREAMED CORN

Serves 6

Ingredients:

2 lbs frozen corn kernels
1 t salt
1¼ c whole milk
4 T unsalted butter
1 c cream cheese, cut into pieces
Freshly ground black pepper to taste

Instructions:

1. Place corn in pressure cooker and add sea salt and fresh ground pepper.
2. Pour milk over corn.
3. Take butter and cream cheese and place over top of the corn. Do not mix.
4. Close lid and lock. Set to "steam/veggies" and adjust for 5 minutes.
5. When done, quick release until all pressure is released.
6. Open and stir gently and thoroughly until all ingredients come together into a creamy consistency.

Vegetables & Sides

OATMEAL

Serves 5

Ingredients:

1¼c steel-cut oats
    (do not use instant)
3¾c water
    Cooking spray

Instructions:

1. Prepare pot to be placed in pressure cooker: spray the insides of it with a good coating.
2. With a paper towel, wipe around edges where the lid seals on pressure cooker.
3. Pour in water and steel-cut oats. Mix.
4. Close lid and lock. Set to "multi grain" for a chewy consistency at 10 minutes; for a creamy consistency, set to 13 minutes.
5. When done, natural release for 35 minutes. Afterward, quick release until all pressure is released.
6. Open carefully and serve.

Tip: If you're not eating oatmeal right after cooking, set pressure cooker to "warm" to keep oatmeal hot. When you set to "multi grain", cooker will stay on "warm" until turned off or unplugged.

Vegetables & Sides

QUINOA & VEGGIES

Serves 4

Ingredients:

- 3 stalks of celery, small dice
- 1 red bell pepper, deveined, seeds removed, and small dice
- 1½c quinoa, uncooked
- ¼t sea salt
- 4c spinach
- 1½c chicken stock
- 2 tomatoes, diced
- ½c black olives, diced
- ⅓c pesto
- ½c feta cheese
- ¼c almonds, sliced

Instructions:

1. Add celery and bell pepper to cooker.
2. Rinse and drain quinoa. Pour quinoa into pot. Add sea salt.
3. Add spinach and chicken stock.
4. Close lid and lock. Set to "rice" and adjust for 3 minutes.
5. When done, natural release for 35 minutes. Afterward, quick release until all pressure is released.
6. Open. Carefully scrape out quinoa. Add tomatoes, olives, pesto, almonds, and feta cheese. Serve.

Vegetables & Sides

QUINOA TABBOULEH

Serves 6

Ingredients:

- 2c   quinoa
- 3c   water
- 2t   sea salt to taste, divided
- 4T   fresh lemon juice, divided
- 2   garlic cloves, finely minced
- 1c   olive oil
       Freshly ground pepper to taste
- 1   large cucumber, quartered, cut into ½-inch pieces
- 2pt   cherry or grape tomatoes, halved
- 1⅓c   chopped parsley
- 1c   chopped mint
- 4   green onions, thinly sliced
- 1-2t mint simple syrup (optional)

Instructions:

1. Rinse quinoa thoroughly. Drain.
2. Add quinoa, water, and ½t of the sea salt to pressure cooker.
3. Close lid and lock. Set to "rice" and adjust for 1 minute.
4. When done, natural release for 35 minutes. Afterward, quick release until all pressure is released.
5. Open and mix in 2T lemon juice and garlic. Allow garlic to soften for 30 minutes.
6. Spread quinoa over a rimmed cookie sheet and allow to cool, about 10 minutes.
7. In a large bowl, whisk together 2T lemon juice, olive oil, and fresh ground pepper. Stir in quinoa and remaining ingredients (except syrup).
8. Season to taste with additional sea salt and fresh ground pepper. Add mint simple syrup (optional) and serve.

Vegetables & Sides

QUINOA

Serves 2

Ingredients:

- 1c quinoa
- 1c chicken broth, vegetable broth, or water

Instructions:

1. Set pressure cooker to "sear" and add quinoa.
2. Toast quinoa for 2-3 minutes, stirring frequently.
3. Add broth or water.
4. Close lid and lock. Set to "rice" and adjust for 3 minutes.
5. When done, natural release for 35 minutes. Afterward, quick release until all pressure is released.
6. Open and serve.

Vegetables & Sides

SOFT-OR HARD-BOILED EGGS

Serves 6

Ingredients:

1 dozen large eggs
1c water

Instructions:

1. Place rack in bottom of pressure cooker and pour in water.
2. Place in 3 to 12 eggs at a time on rack.
3. Close lid and lock. Set to "canning" or "bake".
4. For soft-boiled eggs, set to cook for 4 minutes. For hard-boiled eggs, set for 6 minutes.
5. When cooked, quick release until all pressure is released.
6. Open lid carefully. Allow eggs to cool.

Vegetables & Sides

SOUTHERN GREENS
WITH SMOKED BACON

Serves 6

Ingredients:

- 1 lb collard greens, cleaned, stems trimmed
- ¼ lb smoked bacon, cut into 1-inch pieces
- ½ c water
-   Sea salt and freshly ground black pepper

Instructions:

1. Set to "sear" and add bacon. Cook until brown and crispy. Remove bacon and drain on paper towels.
2. Add collard greens, packing all into pressure cooker. (The max limit is fine as long as you can close lid; when collard greens are cooking they will wilt.)
3. Return bacon to cooker. Sprinkle collards with sea salt and fresh ground pepper. Add water.
4. Close lid and lock. Set to "steam/veggies" and adjust for 10-15 minutes.
5. When done, quick release until all pressure is released.
6. Open and remove collards. Add fresh ground pepper to taste and serve.

Vegetables & Sides

STEAMED SWEET POTATOES
WITH AGAVE NECTAR & SEA SALT

Serves 2

Ingredients:

- 1-4 sweet potatoes (6-7oz each)
- ¼c agave nectar
- 1c water
- Sea salt

Instructions:

1. Place rack on bottom of pressure cooker and add water. Place sweet potatoes on rack.
2. Close lid and lock. Set for "steam/veggies" and adjust for 16 minutes.
3. When done, quick release until all pressure is released.
4. Open and check to see if sweet potatoes are done.
5. Once cooked, cut in half or into ½-inch rounds.
6. Place sweet potatoes on a plate and drizzle agave nectar on top. Season with sea salt.

Tip: Serve sweet potatoes as a savory side dish or as a dessert.

Vegetables & Sides

SWEET ACORN SQUASH

Serves 4

Ingredients:

2	acorn squash, cut into halves
1c	water
4T	butter
2T	raw sugar or agave nectar
½t	nutmeg
	Sea salt

Instructions:

1. Place rack in bottom of pressure cooker and add water.
2. Season acorn squash with sea salt. Arrange cut acorn squash flesh side up on rack.
3. Close lid and lock. Set to "steam/veggies" for 5 minutes.
4. When done, quick release until all pressure is released.
5. Open. Carefully remove acorn squash (they will be hot).
6. Scoop out the flesh from the squash and cut into chunks or mash and add additional ingredients including butter, raw sugar or agave nectar, and nutmeg. Serve warm.

Vegetables & Sides

SWEET & SPICY CABBAGE
WITH CARAWAY

Serves 4

Ingredients:

- 3 lbs white cabbage, divided into 8 wedges
- 1 medium carrot, grated
- ¼c apple cider vinegar
- 1t raw Demerara sugar
- ½t cayenne powder
- ½t red pepper flakes
- 1t caraway
- 2t cornstarch
- 1T sesame seed oil
- 1¼c, plus 2t water, divided

Instructions:

1. Set to "sear", add oil, and brown cabbage wedges on each side for 3 minutes.
2. Once browned, remove cabbage. Add 1¼c of the water, vinegar, Demerara sugar, cayenne, caraway, and red pepper flakes and stir.
3. Return cabbage wedges to cooker and sprinkle grated carrot on top.
4. Close lid and lock. Set to "steam/veggies" for 5 minutes.
5. When done, natural release for 35 minutes. Afterward, quick release until all pressure is released.
6. Open and remove wedges. Arrange on a platter. Keep liquid in the pressure cooker.
7. Set to "sear". Keep lid off.
8. Mix the cornstarch with 2t of the water and pour into pressure cooker. Stir until boiling and/or liquid is thickened.
9. Once thickened, pour sauce on top of cabbage and serve.

Vegetables & Sides

SWEET POTATOES
WITH PECANS & BOURBON

Serves 4

Ingredients:

- 3 sweet potatoes, peeled, cut into ¾-inch slices, and then cubed
- 2T cornstarch
- ½c bourbon
- ½c water
- ¼c sugar
- ¼c light brown sugar
- ¼c maple syrup
- 2T butter
- ½c chopped pecans

Instructions:

1. In a bowl, mix sweet potatoes and cornstarch. Coat evenly.
2. Set to "sear" and add butter.
3. Add sweet potatoes and lightly brown.
4. Pour in bourbon and water. Add sugar, light brown sugar, and maple syrup.
5. Close lid and lock. Set to "potatoes" and adjust for 3 minutes.
6. When done, quick release until all pressure is released.
7. Open and add pecans. Stir and serve.

Vegetables & Sides

WHOLE BABY POTATOES

Serves 4

Ingredients:

- 2 lbs baby potatoes or fingerling potatoes
- 3-4 cloves garlic, minced
- ¼ c chopped parsley
- 3 T butter
- ½ c chicken stock
- 1 t paprika

Instructions:

1. Place potatoes in pressure cooker. Add chicken stock.
2. Close lid and lock. Set to "steam/veggies" and adjust for 3 minutes.
3. When done, quick release until all pressure is released.
4. Open and drain potatoes in a colander; set aside.
5. Clean and wipe down pot.
6. Set to "sear" and add butter. Once butter has melted, return potatoes to cooker. Cook until golden brown.
7. Add garlic and paprika and continue cooking for an additional 2-3 minutes.
8. Top with parsley and serve.

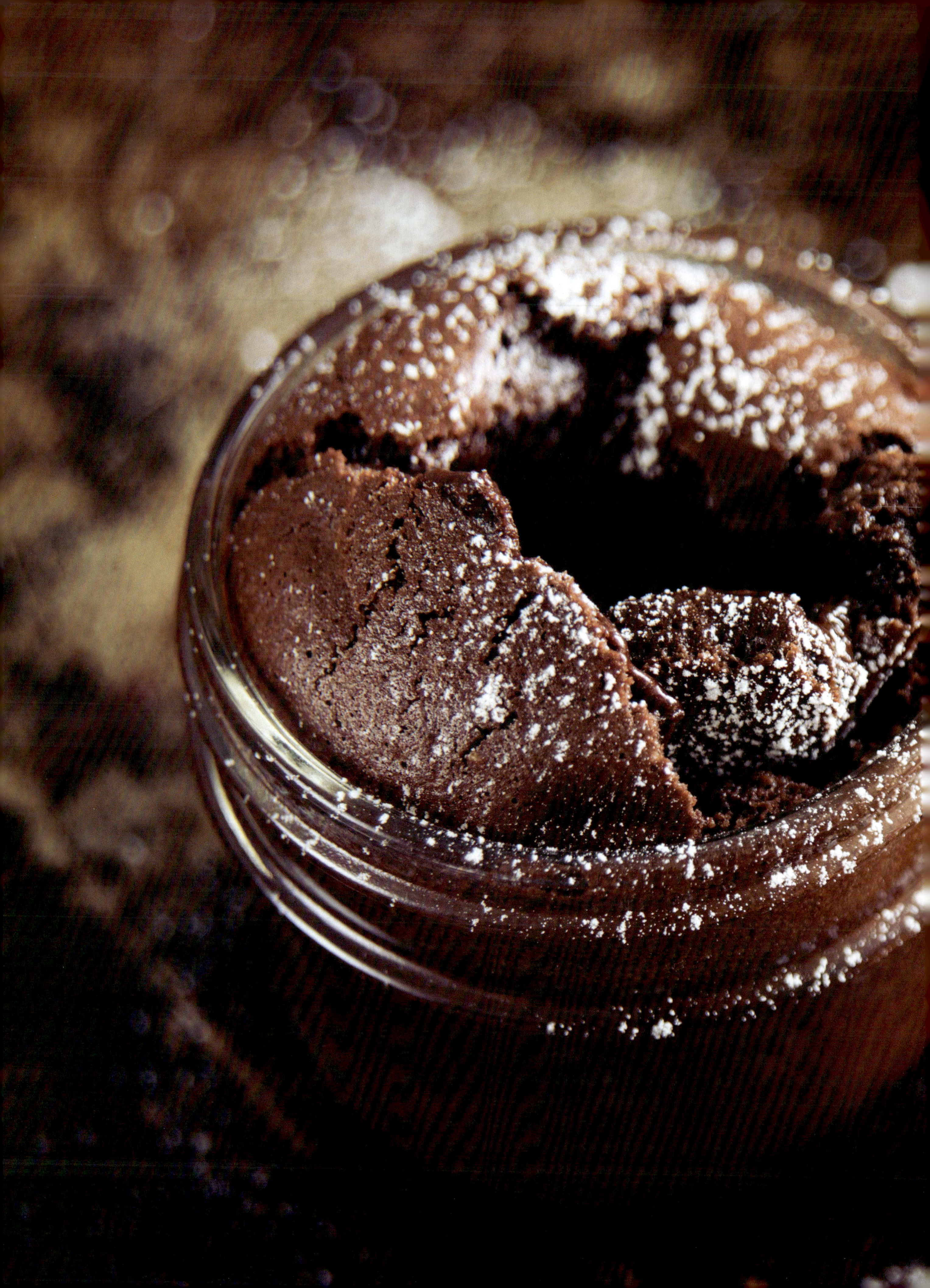

DESSERTS

Apple Cake 248
Breakfast Cake 249
Bread Pudding with Apricots 251
Chocolate Lava Cake 252
Cinnamon Baked Apples 253
Banana French Toast 255
Orange Olive Oil Cake 256
Poached Pears 257
Classic New York Cheesecake 259
Pumpkin Pie 260
Stuffed Peaches 261
Crème Brûlée 263
Key Lime Pie 264
Tapioca Pudding 265
Brownies 267

Desserts

APPLE CAKE

Serves 6

Ingredients:

- 2 apples, peeled, cored, and sliced thin
- 2t cinnamon, ground
- 7-oz pkg. muffin mix
- ½c milk
- 2T sugar
- 2c water
- 1t vegetable oil
- Almond slivers (optional)

Instructions:

1. Add oil to 6-inch pan. Rub oil on bottom and sides of pan.
2. Layer apples along the bottom and slightly up the sides of pan.
3. Sprinkle cinnamon and sugar over apples.
4. Prep muffin mix per directions. Combine with milk.
5. Pour mixture on top of apples.
6. Pour 2c water into cooker and place rack on bottom. Place pan on rack.
7. Close lid and lock. Set to "bake" and adjust for 20 minutes.
8. When done, natural release for 35 minutes. Afterward, quick release until all pressure is released.
9. Open and carefully remove cake. Add almonds on top. Let cool for 10 minutes.

Desserts

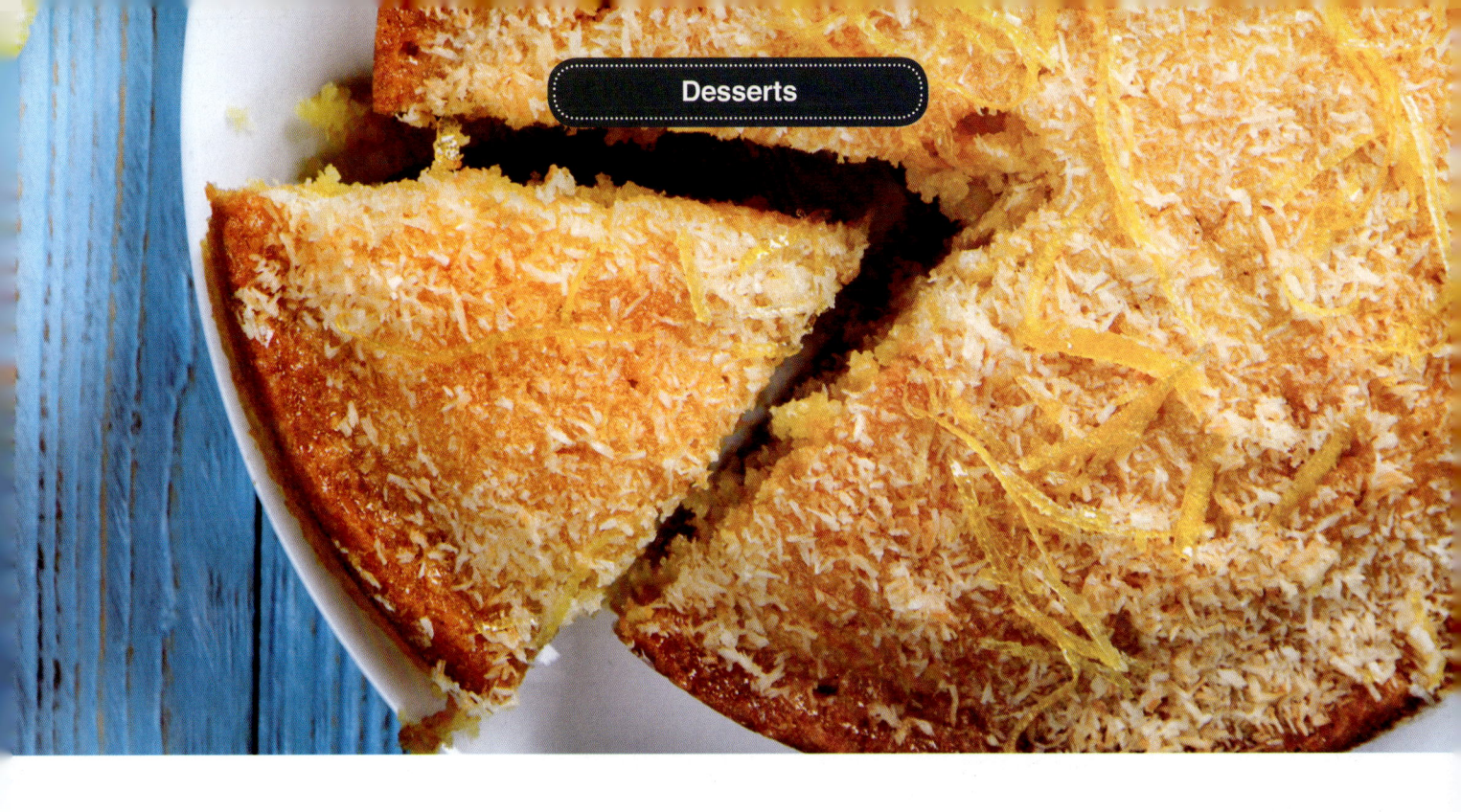

BREAKFAST CAKE

Serves 4

Ingredients:

- 5 eggs
- ¼c sugar
- 2T butter, melted
- ¾c ricotta cheese
- ¾c vanilla yogurt
- 2t vanilla extract
- 1c flour
- ½t sea salt
- 2t baking powder
- ½c berries

Yogurt Glaze:

- ¼c yogurt
- ½t vanilla extract
- 1t milk
- 2T powdered sugar

Instructions:

1. Grease a 7-inch Bundt cake pan.
2. In a bowl, mix eggs and sugar until smooth. Add ricotta, yogurt, butter, and vanilla extract and mix.
3. In another bowl, mix flour, sea salt, and baking powder.
4. Combine flour mixture with egg mixture and pour into greased cake pan. Add in berries on top of the batter.
5. Add 1c of water to cooker and place rack on the bottom. Carefully place pan with batter on rack.
6. Close lid and lock. Set to "bake" and adjust for 25 minutes.
7. While cooking, make yogurt glaze by mixing yogurt, vanilla extract, milk, and powdered sugar in a bowl.
8. When cake is done, natural release, 10 minutes. Afterward, quick release until all pressure is released.
9. Open and remove. Carefully turn the cake and pan over and onto a plate or platter. Lift up pan (use oven gloves, if necessary). Top with yogurt glaze and serve.

Desserts

BREAD PUDDING
WITH APRICOTS

Serves 4

Ingredients:

- 1c   dried apricots, small dice
- 8   slices cinnamon bread, cut into 1-inch cubes
- 3   whole eggs
- 3c   milk
- ½t   ground cinnamon
- 1t   vanilla extract
- ½c   packed brown sugar
- ¼t   sea salt
- 4T   melted unsalted butter

Caramel-pecan sauce:
- ½c   toasted pecans, coarsely chopped
- ¾c   brown sugar
- ¼c   corn syrup
- 2T   unsalted butter
- 2T   heavy cream
- ½t   sea salt
- 1t   vanilla extract

Instructions:

1. In a large bowl, mix eggs, milk, salt, brown sugar, vanilla, and cinnamon. Add apricots and bread to soak in the same bowl. Add melted butter. Stir well and soak for 15 to 20 minutes.
2. Apply butter or non-stick spray to a 1½-qt baking tray.
3. Pour soaked bread mixture in prepared pan. Cover with foil.
4. Add in 1½c of hot water to pressure cooker. Place rack on bottom of cooker.
5. Place the bread pudding on top of rack.
6. Close lid and lock. Set to "bake" and adjust for 20 minutes.
7. When done, quick release until all pressure is released.
8. Open and carefully remove bread pudding. Remove steamer rack.
9. While bread pudding is cooling, make the caramel-pecan sauce: Set cooker to "sear" and combine butter, brown sugar, corn syrup, heavy cream, and sea salt in cooker. Bring up to a boil.
10. Simmer until sauce is smooth, stirring constantly.
11. Stir in vanilla and toasted pecans.

Tip: Serve bread pudding in bowl with sauce on top or on the side.

Desserts

CHOCOLATE LAVA CAKE

Serves 6

Ingredients:

1	stick butter
3	eggs
1	egg yolk
1c	semi-sweet chocolate chips
1T	vanilla extract
6T	flour
1c	powdered sugar

Instructions:

1. Place chocolate chips and butter in a bowl. Heat in the microwave for 2 minutes.
2. Remove and mix well.
3. Mix in the powdered sugar until smooth.
4. Add in eggs, yolk, vanilla extract, and flour.
5. Pour batter into 3-inch soufflé cups.
6. Place cups in pressure cooker.
7. Close lid and lock. Set to "bake" and adjust for 9 minutes.
8. When done, quick release until all pressure is released.
9. Open. Carefully remove cake.
10. Top with choice of ice cream, caramel, etc.

Desserts

CINNAMON BAKED APPLES

Serves 6

Ingredients:

6	apples, cored
¼c	raisins
1c	red wine
½c	sugar
1t	cinnamon powder

Instructions:

1. Place apples onto the bottom of pressure cooker.
2. Pour in wine, sprinkle in raisins, and add sugar and cinnamon.
3. Close lid and lock. Set to "bake" and adjust for 10 minutes.
4. When done, natural release for 35 minutes. Afterward, quick release until all pressure is released.
5. Open. Scoop apples out and serve in a bowl with some of the cooking liquid.

Desserts

BANANA FRENCH TOAST

Serves 2

Ingredients:

6	slices of French bread, sliced
4	bananas, sliced
2T	brown sugar
¼c	cream cheese
3	eggs
½c	milk
1T	sugar
1t	vanilla extract
½t	cinnamon
2T	butter, sliced
¼c	pecans, chopped
¾c	water

Instructions:

1. Grease round, 7-inch baking dish.
2. Add a layer of sliced bread.
3. Layer sliced bananas over bread and sprinkle brown sugar on top.
4. Melt cream cheese in a microwave. Cover bananas with melted cream cheese.
5. Repeat layering process with rest of bread and bananas.
6. Place butter over the top of the bread slices and bananas.
7. In a mixing bowl, beat eggs and whisk in milk and vanilla extract. Add sugar, cinnamon, and pecans.
8. Pour egg mixture over bread and bananas in baking dish.
9. Pour ¾c water in pressure cooker and place rack on the bottom. Place baking dish on top of rack.
10. Close lid and lock. Set to "bake" and adjust for 25 minutes.
11. When done, natural release for 35 minutes. Afterward, quick release until all pressure is released.
12. Open, remove to cool, and serve.

Desserts

ORANGE OLIVE OIL CAKE

Serves 6

Ingredients:

- 1c plain yogurt
- ½c olive oil
- ¾c sugar
- 1t vanilla extract
- Zest of an orange
- 1½c all-purpose flour
- 1¼t baking powder
- ½t baking soda
- 1t orange extract

Instructions:

1. Cut a circle of parchment paper that will fit in the bottom of the pressure cooker's pot; set aside.
2. Close lid and lock. Set to "bake" and adjust for 5 minutes.
3. In a mixing bowl, combine yogurt and sugar. Beat well, removing any lumps. Add baking soda and baking powder. Mix well and let sit for 5 minutes until small bubbles appear on surface of the mixture.
4. Add vanilla extract, orange extract, orange zest, and olive oil. Mix well, then add the flour while sifting it. Gently fold into the mixture.
5. Open cooker. Place parchment paper on the bottom (no need to use a pan, cooking spray, or any grease).
6. Pour batter into cooker on the parchment paper. Use a spatula to spread out evenly.
7. Close lid and lock, (leave the valve open if using pressure cooker with a pressure release switch). Set to "bake" and adjust for 20 minutes.
8. When done, quick release until all pressure is released. Open and let the cake cool down. Remove cake. Slice and serve.

Desserts

POACHED PEARS

Serves 6

Ingredients:

6   pears, peeled
1   bottle of red wine
1   bay leaf
4   whole cloves
1   stick cinnamon
1t ginger, minced
2c sugar

Instructions:

1. Peel pears, leave stems attached.
2. Pour bottle of wine into pressure cooker.
3. Add pears, bay leaf, cloves, cinnamon, ginger, and sugar. Mix well.
4. Close lid and lock. Set to "bake" and adjust for 5-7 minutes.
5. When done, natural release for 35 minutes. Afterward, quick release until all pressure is released.
6. Open and use tongs or large spoon to remove pears.
7. Leave liquid in cooker. Use as syrup to drizzle on pears.

Tip: Serve pears at room temperature or chilled.

Desserts

CLASSIFY NEW YORK CHEESECAKE

Serves 8

Ingredients:

Batter for cheesecake:
- 8oz plain cream cheese
- ⅔c sugar
- 2 large eggs
- ½t vanilla extract
- ¼c sour cream

Crust:
- 2T unsalted butter, melted
- ¾c graham crackers (ground)

Topping:
Cherry, blueberry, or your own favorite pie filling

Instructions:

1. Mix melted butter and graham cracker crumbs.
2. Take a 6-inch springform pan; spray with non-stick coating.
3. Press the graham cracker/butter mixture into pan.
4. For the filling, make sure cream cheese is soft. Mix softened cream cheese in a mixing bowl and beat with sugar for 3 to 5 minutes.
5. Add eggs, one at a time while mixing.
6. Add sour cream and then add vanilla extract.
7. Pour cream cheese mixture into pan with crust.
8. Tap the pan on table to release any air pockets.
9. Cover with foil and place in pressure cooker. Close lid and lock. Set to "bake" and adjust for 35 minutes.
10. When done, natural release for 10 minutes. Afterward, quick release until all pressure is released.
11. Open lid carefully and remove from cooker. Cool overnight in refrigerator, or for 4-5 hours in the refrigerator.
12. Remove cheesecake from pan: run a knife around the wall of pan between wall and crust to release cake from pan. Next, unlatch springform pan and lift up, using both hands.
13. Place cheesecake on serving platter and garnish with fruit filling topping.

Tip: Cut cheesecake with a sharp kitchen knife to easily adjust portions.

Desserts

PUMPKIN PIE

Serves 8

Ingredients:

2lbs pumpkin, diced
1c whole milk
¾c maple syrup
2 eggs
1t powdered cinnamon
½t powdered ginger
¼t powdered cloves
1T cornstarch
Pinch of sea salt

Optional garnish:
Whipped cream
Chopped pecans

Instructions:

1. Add 1c water to pressure cooker.
2. Place pumpkin cubes in a steamer basket or rack and set in cooker.
3. Close lid and lock. Set to "steam/veggies" and adjust for 3-4 minutes.
4. When done, quick release until all pressure is released.
5. In a mixing bowl, add milk, maple syrup, eggs, cinnamon, ginger, cloves, sea salt, and cornstarch. Mix well.
6. Remove pumpkin from cooker. In a bowl, blend egg mixture and pumpkin together.
7. Pour mixture into 7-inch cooking pan. Place rack in bottom of cooker. Place pan with mixture on the rack in cooker. Add water to cooker if necessary.
8. Close lid and lock. Set to "bake" and adjust for 8-10 minutes.
9. When done, natural release for 35 minutes. Afterward, quick release until all pressure is released.
10. Open and carefully remove pie. Let pie cool before serving, or refrigerate for up to two days.

Desserts

STUFFED PEACHES

Serves 5

Ingredients:

5	peaches
¼c	flour
¼c	sugar
2T	butter, softened
½t	ground cinnamon
¼t	almond extract
	Pinch sea salt
1c	water

Instructions:

1. Using a paring knife, carefully slice the tops off peaches in a circular motion. Make a cut into each peach down the center and inside of the flesh and then around the pit. Remove pit with a spoon.
2. In a bowl, mix flour, sugar, butter, cinnamon, almond extract, and sea salt to make crumble.
3. Spoon crumble mixture into hollowed out holes in all peaches.
4. Pour water into cooker and place rack on bottom. Place peaches on rack.
5. Close lid and lock. Set to "bake" and adjust for 4 minutes.
6. When done, quick release until all pressure is released.
7. Open and carefully remove peaches. Allow to cool.

Tip: Serve peaches warm with vanilla ice cream.

Desserts

CRÈME BRÛLÉE

Serves 6

Ingredients:

- 8 egg yolks
- ⅓c granulated sugar, plus 1t for caramelizing
- 2c heavy cream
- 1½t vanilla extract
- Pinch of sea salt
- 1½c water

Instructions:

1. Add 1½c water to pressure cooker. Place rack on the bottom.
2. In a bowl, mix egg yolks with sugar and pinch of sea salt.
3. Add in heavy cream and vanilla extract. Whisk until blended well.
4. Strain into a wet measuring cup with a spout.
5. Pour mixture into 6 custard cups. Cover with foil.
6. Place filled cups on rack in pressure cooker.
7. Close lid and lock. Set to "bake" and adjust for 6 minutes.
8. When done, natural release 10 minutes, then quick release until all pressure is released.
9. Open and remove each. Allow each crème brûlée to cool.
10. Place each on a tray and wrap in plastic. Refrigerate for at least 2 hours.
11. When ready to serve, remove from fridge and sprinkle each with 1t of white granulated sugar.
12. Take a small culinary torch and make a flame 2 inches above each custard surface, moving in a circular motion to melt sugar and to caramelize the top.

KEY LIME PIE

Serves 6

Ingredients:

Crust:
- ¾c graham cracker crumbs (5 crackers)
- 3T unsalted butter, melted
- 1T sugar

Filling:
- 1 can sweetened condensed milk
- 4 egg yolks
- ½c key lime juice
- ⅓c sour cream
- 2T key limes (zest only)

Instructions:

1. For the crust, mix graham crackers, melted butter, and sugar in a bowl.
2. Press mixture into a 7-inch pie pan.
3. Place in freezer for 10 minutes.
4. For the filling, in a mixing bowl, beat the egg yolks until they are a light yellow, gradually beating in the sweetened condensed milk.
5. Add lime juice and mix until smooth. Stir in sour cream and zest.
6. Remove pie crust from freezer. Pour batter into pan on top of the crust.
7. Pour 1c water into pressure cooker, put rack on bottom, and place pie on top.
8. Close lid and lock. Set to "bake" and adjust for 15 minutes.
9. When done, natural release, 10 minutes. Afterward, quick release until all pressure is released.
10. Open. Remove pie and let cool.
11. Cover pie with plastic. Place in fridge to chill for 4 hours.

Desserts

TAPIOCA PUDDING

Serves 2

Ingredients:

½c small tapioca pearls
1½c water
½c whole milk
½c sugar
¼t sea salt
2   egg yolks
½t vanilla extract

Instructions:

1. Mix tapioca and water together.
2. Pour in pressure cooker.
3. Close lid and lock. Set to "steam/veggies" and adjust for 6 minutes.
4. When done, natural release for 35 minutes. Afterward, quick release until all pressure is released.
5. Open and whisk sugar and sea salt into tapioca.
6. In a small bowl, whisk egg yolks and milk.
7. Pour egg mixture through mesh strainer and into the tapioca.
8. Set to "sear" and cook, stirring constantly until boiling.
9. Turn off pressure cooker and stir in vanilla extract.
10. Cool to room temperature.
11. Pour into individual serving dishes and chill in refrigerator.

Desserts

BROWNIES

Serves 4

Ingredients:

- ½c butter
- ¼c cocoa powder
- 1c sugar
- ¾c unbleached white flour
- ¾t baking powder
- ¼t sea salt
- 1T honey
- 2   eggs
- 1c water
- ½c walnuts (optional)

Instructions:

1. In a saucepan on low heat, add butter and melt. Mix in the cocoa powder.
2. In a bowl, combine sugar, flour, baking powder, and sea salt. Mix well.
3. Add honey to dry flour mixture, then eggs. Add melted butter and cocoa mixture to bowl. Add in walnuts (optional).
4. Pour mixture into greased pan (must fit into cooker).
5. Add 1c water to pressure cooker. Place rack on the bottom.
6. Place pan with mixture onto rack in cooker.
7. Close lid and lock. Set to "bake" and adjust for 35 minutes.
8. When done, natural release for 35 minutes. Afterward, quick release until all pressure is released.
9. Open. Remove brownies and allow to cool.
10. Cut brownies and serve.

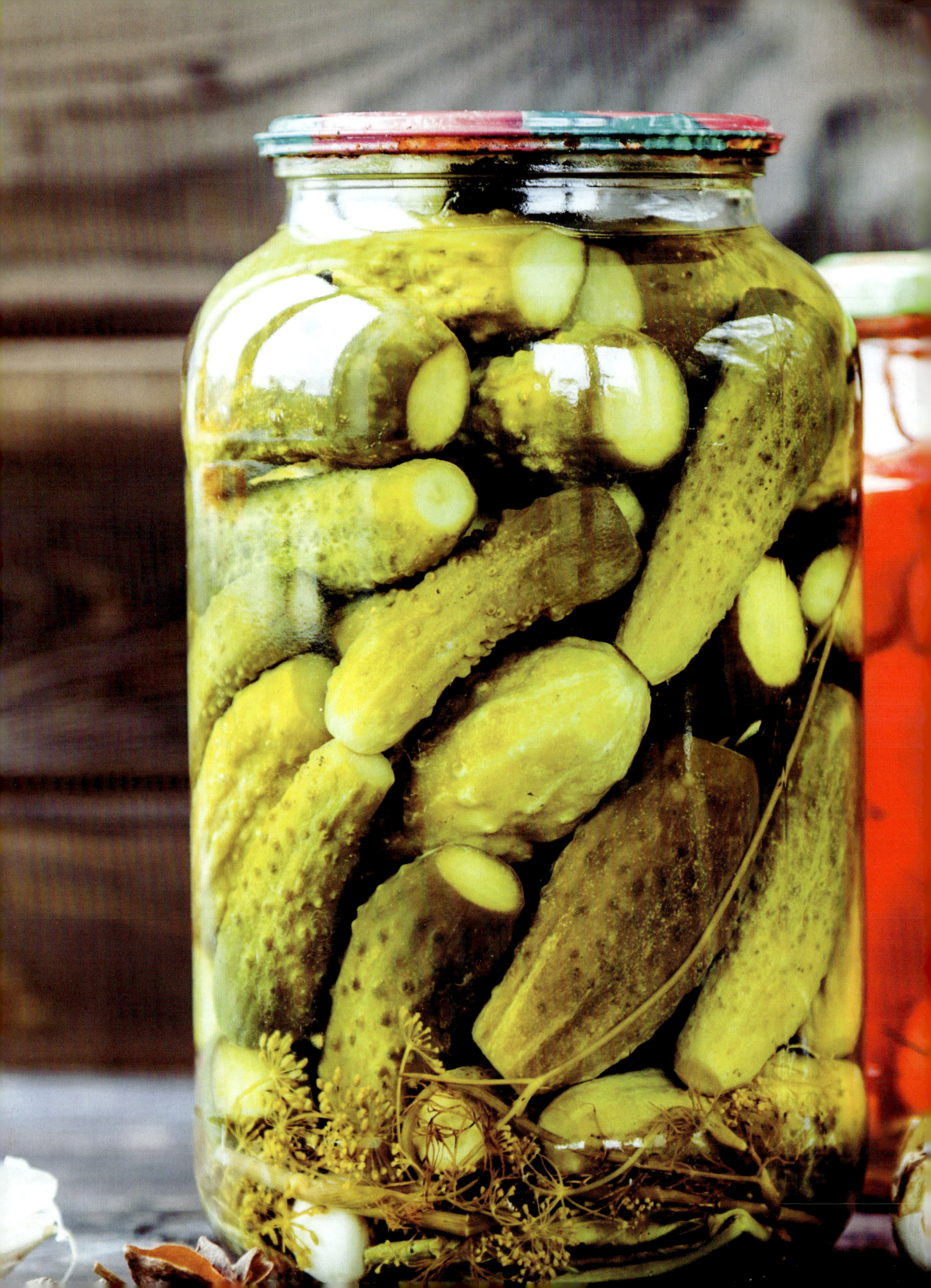

CANNING

Apple Butter 272
Apple Sauce 273
Candied Garlic 274
Dulce de Leche 275
Giardiniera 276
Homemade Vegetable Juice 277
Lemon Curd 278
Peaches with Agave 279
Refrigerator Pickles 280
Tomato Salsa 281

Canning

APPLE BUTTER

Serves 6

Ingredients:

- 16 apples, cored, sliced
- ½c cider vinegar
- 2½c brown sugar
- 3t cinnamon
- ¼t ground cloves

Instructions:

1. Place apples and cider vinegar in pressure cooker.
2. Close lid and lock. Set to "bake" and adjust for 1½ hours.
3. When done, natural release for 35 minutes. Afterward, quick release until all pressure is released.
4. Open and remove apples. Transfer apples to blender or food processor. Process or blend until smooth.
5. Transfer mixture to pressure cooker. Add brown sugar and spices.
6. Close lid and lock. Set to "bake" for an additional 30 minutes.
7. When done, natural release for 35 minutes. Afterward, quick release until all pressure is released.
8. Open and stir (apple butter will seem watery, but will thicken).
9. Transfer apple butter into canning jars.
10. After apple butter has cooled in jars, cover with lids and proceed with canning as directed.

Tip: You can either refrigerate, freeze, or can, according to specific canning directions.

Canning

APPLE SAUCE

Serves 6

Ingredients:

- 10 large Jonagold apples, peeled, cored, and quartered or sliced
- ¼c apple juice or water
- ¼c sugar
- 1t ground cinnamon

Instructions:

1. Place apple pieces, apple juice, sugar, and cinnamon into pressure cooker. Stir to combine.
2. Close lid and lock. Set to "steam/veggies" and adjust for 4 minutes.
3. When done, natural release for 35 minutes. Afterward, quick release until all pressure is released.
4. Open. With an immersion blender, break up large chunks until you've achieved desired consistency. Or, stir well with spoon for long period until chunks have broken up well.
5. Transfer apple sauce into canning jars.
6. After apple sauce has cooled, cover with lids and proceed, following canning directions.

Tip: You can either refrigerate, freeze, or can, according to canning directions.

Canning

CANDIED GARLIC

Serves 4

Ingredients:

1c sugar
1c orange juice
2c garlic cloves, peeled

Instructions:

1. Set to "sear" and pour orange juice and sugar into cooker. Bring to a boil.
2. Add garlic cloves to mixture. Cook down until liquid has reduced.
3. Place cooked garlic into canning jars.
4. Follow all instructions for canning.

Canning

DULCE DE LECHE

Serves 4

Ingredients:

2   cans sweetened condensed milk
3   half-pt, wide-mouth canning jars (makes 24oz)
1½c water

Instructions:

1. Pour sweetened condensed milk into jars, evenly distributed. Leave levels 1 inch from the top of the jars.
2. Remove air by tapping jars on counter, place lids on jars, and tighten. Follow canning directions.
3. Place rack on bottom of pressure cooker. Fill bottom of pressure cooker with 1½c water.
4. Place jars on the rack.
5. Close lid and lock. Set to "canning" and adjust for 40 minutes.
6. When done, quick release until all pressure is released.
7. Open, remove jars, and cool for 30 minutes.
8. Place jars in refrigerator.

Canning

GIARDINIERA

Serves 6-8

Ingredients:

- 8 jalapeños, sliced (serranos substituted, for more heat)
- ½ large cauliflower, cut into florets
- 2 carrots, diced
- 2 celery stalks, diced
- 1 green bell pepper, diced
- 1 red bell pepper, diced
- 2 sweet banana peppers, diced
- 1 sweet onion, diced
- ½c sea salt
- 3 cloves garlic, whole
- 2½t dried oregano
- 1t red pepper flakes
- ½t celery seeds
- Freshly ground black pepper
- ½c cider vinegar
- ½c white vinegar
- ½c extra-virgin olive oil
- ½c vegetable/canola oil

Instructions:

1. Combine vegetables and salt in a non-reactive container. Add enough water to cover contents.
2. Stir, cover, and refrigerate for at least 12 hours.
3. Strain vegetables from brine. Rinse well; set aside.
4. In a large glass bowl, add remaining seasonings.
5. Add vinegars and stir until mixed well.
6. Whisk mixture while incorporating the oils.
7. Add the reserved, brined vegetables into mixture. Gently stir until vegetables are well-coated.
8. Refrigerate giardiniera for 48 hours before serving. Giardiniera may be left covered in the bowl or transferred to clean jars.

Tips: If giardiniera isn't canned in pressure cooker, it must be stored in the refrigerator, where it will keep for a few weeks. If canning, follow all directions.

Serves 4 per jar.

Canning

HOMEMADE VEGETABLE JUICE

Serves 6

Ingredients:

- 15lbs ripe tomatoes, diced (8qts)
- 1 large bell pepper, small dice
- 2 large onions, small dice
- 1½c diced celery
- 2 bay leaves
- 12 fresh basil leaves (or 2t dried basil)
- 2t prepared horseradish
- ½t freshly ground black pepper
- 3t sugar
- 2t Worcestershire sauce
- ½c lemon juice

Instructions:

1. Place all ingredients (except lemon juice) in cooker.
2. Close lid and lock. Set to "bake" and adjust for 45 minutes.
3. When done, natural release for 35 minutes. Afterward, quick release until all pressure is released.
4. Open. All vegetables should be soft when stirring using a spoon.
5. Remove vegetables and press through a fine sieve or food mill.
6. Return strained juice to cooker. Stir in lemon juice and bring up to a boil.
7. Turn off heat. Cool to room temperature.
8. Transfer vegetable juice to airtight containers and store in refrigerator or can the juice.*

*If canning, use specified jars and follow all canning directions. Each jar contains 2 servings of juice.

Canning

LEMON CURD

Serves 12

Ingredients:

6T	unsalted butter, softened
1c	sugar
2	eggs
⅔c	lemon juice
1-2t	lemon zest
3	half-pint mason jars

Instructions:

1. In a bowl, mix butter and sugar for 2 minutes.
2. Slowly add in eggs and mix for 1 minute.
3. Add lemon juice and lemon zest. Pour mixture into mason jars, evenly distributed. Leave levels 1 inch from the top of the jar.
4. Remove air by tapping jars on counter, and close lids.
5. Place rack in bottom of pressure cooker and pour in 1½c of water in the bottom. Place jars on rack.*
6. Close lid and lock. Set to "canning" and adjust for 10 minutes.
7. When done, quick release until all pressure is released.
8. Open and remove. Allow curd to cool for 25 minutes.
9. Place in fridge overnight.

*Serves 4 per jar.

Canning

PEACHES
WITH AGAVE

Serves 6

Ingredients:

- 4 peaches, peeled, halved (4c)
- 1T water
- 1t vanilla extract
- ½T cornstarch
- 1T water
- ¼c agave

Instructions:

1. Set to "sear" and add halved peaches, agave, water, and vanilla extract.
2. Close lid and lock. Set to "steam/veggies" and adjust for 1 minute.
3. When done, natural release, 5 minutes.
4. Afterward, quick release until all pressure is released.
5. In a small bowl, mix cornstarch and remaining 1T of water.
6. Open cooker and set to "sear" again. Pour in cornstarch mixture, whisking continually until thick, about 1 minute.
7. Allow to cool.
8. Remove and pour into canning jars. Follow canning directions.

Canning

REFRIGERATOR PICKLES

Serves 16

Ingredients:

- 10 pickling cucumbers, cut into spears
- 6 cloves garlic, smashed
- 2c water
- 2c white vinegar
- ¼c sea salt
- 1 bunch fresh dill
- 1T pickling spice
- 4 US pint jars with lids

Instructions:

1. Pour water, vinegar, sea salt, pickling spice, garlic, and dill into cooker. Set to "sear" and bring up to a boil.
2. Turn off cooker and allow brine to cool to room temperature.
3. While cooling, place cut pickling cucumber spears into the jars.
4. Strain the spices out of the cooled brine.
5. Carefully pour brine into jars 1 inch from the top.
6. Using a flexible, nonporous spatula, gently press between the pickles and the jar wall to release any trapped air bubbles.
7. Follow canning directions and seal all jars.*

*Serves 4 per jar.

Canning

TOMATO SALSA

Serves 6-8

Ingredients:

- 14 medium-sized tomatoes, washed
- 3c onions, small dice
- ½c jalapeños, minced
- 1c green pepper, small dice
- ½c vinegar
- ½c tomato sauce
- 3T sea salt
- 1T chili powder
- 1T garlic powder
- 1½T cumin
- 5 cloves garlic, peeled, minced
- 1c water

Instructions:

1. Place tomatoes in a pot of boiling water and blanch for 1 minute, then remove and shock tomatoes, dipping them in cold water.
2. Pull off skins of each. Remove core.
3. Place in cooker.
4. Add remaining ingredients and 1c water.
5. Close lid and lock. Set to "steam/veggies" and adjust for 8 minutes.
6. When done, natural release for 35 minutes. Afterward, quick release until all pressure is released.
7. Open and allow to cool.
8. Place tomato salsa into airtight jars.* Or, follow canning directions if storing longer.

*Serves 4 per jar.

INDEX

Beef:
- Barbacoa Beef 101
- BBQ-Style Tri-Tip Beef 104
- Borscht 33
- Bone Broth for Health 11
- Beef Barley Soup 10
- Beef Burgundy with Root Vegetables & Red Wine .. 39
- Beef Cheeks with Carrots 107
- Beef Osso Buco with Gremolata 123
- Beef Tips with Onions & Mushrooms 109
- Beef Stroganoff with Egg Noodles 108
- Brisket 105
- British Pot Roast 112
- Corned Beef & Cabbage 136
- Cuban Ropa Vieja 143
- Italian Beef 141
- Jamaican-Style Oxtail 144
- Korean Short Ribs 151
- Lengua (Beef Tongue) in Salsa Verde 161
- My Mom's Meatloaf 152
- Picadillo 157
- Rigatoni Bolognese 79
- Slow-Braised Brisket with BBQ Sauce 170
- Swedish Meatballs in Gravy 181
- Stuffed Flank Steak 158
- Texas Beef Chili 37
- Tri-Tip Beef in Mushroom Red Wine Sauce 175
- Veal Blanquette 179
- Veal Osso Buco 182
- Yankee Pot Roast with Cider 184
- Yankee Pot Roast with Mushrooms 165

Beans:
- 7-Bean Chili 63
- Black Bean Soup with Cotija Cheese 25
- Black Beans with Chorizo 57
- Black Bean Soup with Toasted Cumin & Cilantro .. 29
- Black-Eyes Peas & Rice 60
- Boston Baked Beans 209
- Red Beans & Rice 87
- Refried Beans 85
- Hoppin' John 75

Canning:
- Apple Butter 270
- Apple Sauce 271
- Candied Garlic 272
- Dulce De Leche 273
- Giardiniera 274
- Homemade Vegetable Rice 275
- Lemon Curd 276
- Peaches with Agave 277
- Refrigerator Pickles 278
- Tomato Salsa 279

Corn:
- Corn & Mushroom Soup 47
- Corn on the Cob 216
- Cornbread 217
- New England-Style Creamed Corn 234

Cheese:
- Nacho Cheese Sauce for Game Day 21

Chicken:
- Arroz Con Pollo (Rice with Chicken) 59
- Balsamic Chicken Thighs 100
- Braised Chicken with White Wine & Olives 111
- Chicken Breasts in Balsamic-Dijon Sauce 185
- Chicken Burrito Bowls 116
- Chicken Soup with Farro & Vegetables 23
- Chicken & Dumpling Soup 41
- Chicken Tortilla Soup 49
- Chicken Alfredo 115
- Chicken Fajitas 117
- Chicken Adobo 120
- Chicken Pot Pie 124
- Chicken Puttanesca 125
- Chorizo & Chicken with Cuban Rice 127
- Chicken Tikka Masala 128
- Chicken Tinga From Mexico 129
- Chicken Cacciatore (Hunter Style) 131
- Chicken with Coconut Curry 132
- Chicken with Italian Seasoning 133
- Chicken Mole 135
- Creamy Chicken Penne 69
- Cream of Chicken with Wild Rice 15
- Indian Butter Chicken 140
- Kung Pao Chicken 155
- Lemon-Butter Chicken with Fresh Herbs 149
- Orange Chicken 156
- Southern-Style Smothered Chicken 171
- Soft- or Hard-Boiled Eggs 239
- Slow-Cooked Buffalo Chicken Wings 169
- Whole Braised Chicken with Sriracha 183
- Pho Ga 45
- Tom Ka Gai 53

Chickpeas:
- Chickpea Hummus 61
- Chickpea Madras Curry 215
- Chickpeas with Tomatoes 35

Desserts:
- Apple Cake 248
- Banana French Toast 255
- Bread Pudding with Apricots 251
- Brownies 267
- Chocolate Lava Cake 252
- Cinnamon Baked Apples 253
- Classic New York Cheesecake 259
- Crème Brûlée 263
- Key Lime Pie 264
- Orange Olive Oil Cake 256
- Poached Pears 257
- Pumpkin Pie 260
- Stuffed Peaches 261
- Tapioca Pudding 265

Grain:
- Basmati Rice with Lemongrass 56
- Bulgur Wheat Pilaf 64

282

INDEX

Couscous with Diced Vegetables & Curry 65
Cuban Rice 71
Dirty Rice 68
Farro 72
Fried Rice 225
Israeli Couscous 73
Jasmine Rice with Sesame Seeds 76
Kale Risotto 77
Mushroom Risotto 83
Polenta with Mascarpone 81
Sesame-Ginger Rice with Broccoli 89
Wild Rice from Minnesota 93
Wild Rice with Pecans & Chives 97
Lentil Soup 44
Oatmeal 235
Quinoa 238
Quinoa Tabbouleh 237
Quinoa & Veggies 236

Ham:
Easter Ham 137
Split Pea Soup with Ham 31
Tuscan White Bean Soup with Swiss chard
& smoked ham 13

Lamb:
Braised Lamb Shanks with Root Vegetables 119
Navarin of Lamb 153

Pasta:
Ditalini with Zucchini & Tomatoes 67
Mac & Cheese 96
Orzo Pasta with Slow-Cooked Lamb 80
Spicy Indian Dal 95
Vegetarian Green Pozole 92
Ziti with Sausage Ragu 91
Ditalini Soup 52

Pastry:
Crustless Cuban Egg Quiche 219
Breakfast Cake 249

Pork:
Asian Braised Pork with Chilies & Ginger 103
Cider-Braised Pork Stew 139
Green Chili Pork Stew 145
Green Chili Pulled Pork Carnitas 147
Kalua Pig 148
Pork Belly with Chinese Spices 159
Pork Chops in Buttermilk Sauce 173
Pork Pozole with Hominy 22
Pork Shanks with Beer & Fennel Seeds 167
Pozole Verde 223
Pulled Pork Carnitas 163
Sugo Maille (Braised Pork Sauce) 174
Stout Beer BBQ Ribs 177
Southern Greens with Smoked Bacon 240

Potatoes:
Baked Potatoes 208
Cheesy Potatoes Au Gratin 213
Creamless Cauliflower Soup with Yukon Potatoes .. 18
Diced Potatoes 220
Potato Leek Soup 38
Real Butter Mashed Potatoes 227
Warm German Potato Salad 231
Whole Baby Potatoes 245

Sausage:
Italian Wedding Soup with Baby Meatballs 19
Sausage & Peppers 162

Seafood:
Bouillabaisse with Rouille Sauce 191
Bourbon Street Gumbo with Shrimp & Andouille 34
Cajun Shrimp Boil 188
Classic Clam Chowder with New Potatoes 14
Gulf Coast Seafood Gumbo 199
Halibut Poached in Lemon & Butter 189
Mustard-Glazed Salmon with Chives 192
Portuguese Fish Stew 193
Rhode Island Steamed Clams 196
San Francisco Bay Cioppino 195
Salmon with Cilantro-Lime Adobo 197
Sesame Steamed Mussels 200
Shrimp Creole 201
Soup of the Seven Seas 50
Spanish Seafood Paella 203
Swordfish, Nonna Gina Style 204
Tuscan-Style Shrimp Scampi 205

Tomatoes:
Marinara Sauce (Traditional) 27
Minestrone Soup 30
Tomato Basil Bisque with Herb Croutons 51

Turkey:
Butter-Braised Turkey Breast 113
Braised Turkey Thighs with
Yukon Gold Potatoes & Cranberries 121
Turkey Soup (From Thanksgiving Leftovers) 17
Turkey Osso Buco with Onions & Tomatoes 178

Vegetables:
Butternut Squash Soup 42
Braised Beets with Pickling Spices 212
Braised Red Cabbage with Vinegar & Red Wine .. 211
Carrot-Ginger Soup 26
Eggplant & Squash Ratatouille 221
Fresh Sage Spaghetti Squash 224
Glazed Root Vegetables 228
Kale with Lemon, Garlic, & Poppy Seeds 232
Marsala Mushrooms 233
Steamed Sweet Potatoes with
Agave Nectar & Sea Salt 241
Sweet Acorn Squash 242
Sweet & Spicy Cabbage with Caraway 243
Sweet Potatoes with Pecans & Bourbon 244
Homemade Vegetable Soup 43
Honey-Glazed Carrots with Almonds 229

NuWave Brio® 6-Qt Digital Air Fryer

Super-heated air cooks your food to crispy, tender perfection. The digital touch screen gives you precise temperature control.

NuWave Medley® Digital Skillet XL

Coated with Duralon® Healthy Ceramic Non-Stick coating for easy cleanup. Includes a premium, vented, tempered glass lid.

NuWave Oven® Pro Plus

Cook healthier meals faster and more efficiently with Triple Combo Cooking Power.

NuWave PIC®

Cook faster, safer, and more efficiently than you ever could on your gas or electric stovetop.